JRPRISE, SECURITY, AND THE
AMERICAN EXPERIENCE

The Joanna Jackson Goldman Memorial Lectures
on American Civilization and Government

# SURPRISE, SECURITY,

## AND THE

# AMERICAN EXPERIENCE

## John Lewis Gaddis

HARVARD UNIVERSITY PRESS

Cambridge, Massachusetts, and London, England     2004

This book is based on lectures that were given at the New York Public Library's Humanities and Social Sciences Library as part of The Joanna Jackson Goldman Memorial Lectures on American Civilization and Government. Made possible by a gift from the Estate of Eric F. Goldman, the lectures and this book are intended to stimulate discussion of contemporary issues that have a long-term significance for American democracy.

Library of Congress Cataloging-in-Publication Data

Gaddis, John Lewis.

Surprise, security, and the American experience / John Lewis Gaddis.

p. cm.—(Joanna Jackson Goldman memorial lectures on American civilization and government)

ISBN 0-674-01174-0 (cloth : alk. paper)

1. United States—Foreign relations. 2. Surprise (Military science)—United States—History. 3. United States—Foreign reations—Philosophy. 4. National security—United States. 5. Strategy. 6. Unilateral acts (International law) 7. Preemptive attack (Military science) I. Title. II. Series.

E183.7.G27 2004      355′.033073—dc22

2003056935

For

Paul Kennedy, Charles Hill,

and the Yale Grand Strategy students

# ACKNOWLEDGMENTS

These essays originated as the 2002 Joanna Jackson Goldman Memorial Lectures at the New York Public Library. I should like to thank the Eric F. Goldman Estate as well as President Paul LeClerc, Public Education Program Manager Betsy Bradley, and their colleagues at the library for making them possible. My colleague Daniel Kevles of the Yale History Department first persuaded me to undertake this project and has been a valued counselor throughout.

My thanks as well, for reading and commenting on drafts of these lectures and the resulting book, to Toni Dorfman, Sulmaan Khan, Melvyn P. Leffler, Norman Naimark, Gaddis Smith, Jeremi Suri, and Jonathan Winkler, along with two anonymous readers for Harvard University Press. Joyce Seltzer and Susan Wallace Boehmer, also of the Press, very efficiently handled the transition from lectures to published volume.

Portions of Chapter 4 originally appeared as "A Grand Strategy of Transformation" in the November/December 2002 issue of *Foreign Policy* and are included here by permission of the publisher, the Carnegie Endowment for International Peace.

The dedication is my way of appreciating two close friends and the students all three of us teach each Monday afternoon at Yale. I can think of no better forum anywhere within which to have debated the implications of September 11, 2001. Finally, I should like to express special gratitude—and deep respect—to my students Lien-Hang Nguyen, Ewan Macdougall, and Schuyler Schouten for what they taught me on the memorable occasions that begin and end this book.

John Lewis Gaddis
New Haven, Connecticut
September 2003

# CONTENTS

# 1

## A MORADING AT YALE

It's in the nature of great surprises in history that you'll always remember where you were when you heard the news.

This is because for most of us most of the time historical and personal experiences don't intersect. We can all see the importance of developments like the collapse of the Soviet Union, or the rise of Islamic fundamentalism, or the emergence of the United States as the most disproportionately powerful state since the Roman empire, but these developments rarely affect the way we get up in the morning, go to work, fall in love, raise families, and grow old. It's hard to see how great events are going to change *us*, even if it's clear that they're going to change the world. The lives we lead go on pretty much as before regardless of what chapter we've entered, or left behind, in the history of our times.

Every now and then, though, historical and personal trajectories do intersect. What causes them to do so is an event that's sufficiently dramatic in the way it happens, sufficiently sweeping in its implications, and—most of all—sufficiently unexpected, that it causes us all to drop whatever it is we're doing and glue ourselves to the global equivalent of the old town crier, CNN. The distinction between the historical and the personal disappears. Some such events—for example, the *Challenger* disaster of 1986, the fall of the Berlin Wall in 1989, the death of Princess Diana in 1997, or the *Columbia* disaster of 2003—will hold our attention for a few days, but life will then more or less return to normal. The convergence of the historical and the personal turns out to be fleeting. The year in which the event took place may remain in our memory, but the specific date probably will not.

Less frequently, surprises produce more lasting linkages between the historical and the personal. You can tell the difference by how we remember: whether by the year, or by the day. Hardly anyone has forgotten that the assassination of President John F. Kennedy took place on November 22, 1963. The day itself has come to stand for something, so that whatever else may have happened on any of the other November 22nds in history, there's no comparison with this one. The same was true of the attack on Pearl Harbor on December 7, 1941. The everyday lives of everyone changed as a result of that event, so that particular December 7th eclipses all the others. September 11, 2001, before the morning had even ended, attained a similar status in our minds. We all remember what we were doing when we heard the news. And we will remember it all over again, when future September 11ths roll around, for the rest of our lives.

What I will recall about that morning is my frustration at being where I was, although in retrospect I'm not sure where else I would rather have been. With two Yale History Department colleagues, I was just about to begin the PhD oral examination of a brilliant Vietnamese-American student, who with her family had fled South Vietnam a quarter century earlier. This was the most critical moment of all her years in graduate school: we would be deciding, on the basis of her performance during the next two hours, whether she would be allowed to proceed to the writing of a dissertation. We knew only, as she entered the room, that something horrible had happened at the World Trade Center. Because we also knew that our student had family in New York, we agreed to say nothing about this news, for fear of rattling her during the examination.

We were, thus, sequestered from 9:30 to 11:30 A.M., although one or another of us was able to slip out from time to time to pick up scraps of information: that a second plane had crashed into the second tower, that a third had gone down somewhere in Washington, that there were an unknown number of other planes in the air headed for an unknown number of destinations. We did the best we could—while worrying whether our own families, friends, or campus might be one of those destinations—to ask the usual sorts of questions one asks in such exams, and our student, very poised, did fine in answering them. We finally ended the ordeal and sent her out of the room, congratulated ourselves on having kept the news from her, and then called her back in to let her know that that she had passed easily. Only at that point did we tell her what had been happening. "Oh, I knew about it," she replied, "but I hadn't wanted to say anything because it might have upset the three of you."

So even though I couldn't be an eyewitness—by way of live television—to the Twin Towers coming down on that dreadful morning, I would not now want to have been anywhere other than where I was. For what my colleagues and I were doing as part of our everyday lives seems to me worth having made the effort to finish up, even as we all knew before we left the examination room that none of our lives would ever be the same. History happens to historians, just as it does to everyone else.

Through the days, weeks, and months that followed, most of us—at least those of us fortunate enough not to have lost loved ones or livelihoods as a result of the attacks—managed to return to an approximation of normality. And yet, our understanding of what is "normal" is not what it once was. Just as New Yorkers go about their familiar activities in the shadow of an unfamiliar skyline, so something within each of us has also changed. It's as if we were all irradiated, on that morning of September 11, 2001, in such a way as to shift our psychological makeup—the DNA in our minds—with consequences that will not become clear for years to come.

It is, therefore, presumptuous to speculate about those consequences so soon after the event, but it's also necessary. For although the *accuracy* of historical writing diminishes as it approaches the present—because perspectives are shorter and there are fewer sources to work with than in treatments of the more distant past—the *relevance* of such writing increases. We act in the present with a view to shaping the future only on the basis of what we know from the past. So we might as well try to know our recent history as best we can, however imperfect the exercise may be. An incomplete map is better than no map at all.

That, then, is what I would like these essays to be: an admittedly premature effort to treat, as history, an event that remains inescapably part of our present—and of our future as well.

# 2

# THE NINETEENTH CENTURY

One of the privileges of moving to Yale was the opportunity to get to know, in the last years of his life, my much missed History Department colleague C. Vann Woodward. Vann made his career as one of the most distinguished historians of the American South; in 1959, however, at the height of the Cold War, he briefly but with his usual breadth took up a different subject: the relationship between security and the American character. Just as the frontier historian Frederick Jackson Turner over half a century earlier had linked the culture and institutions of the United States to the availability throughout most of its history of mostly free land, so Woodward argued that historians should also connect these to the availability of mostly free security. That great benefit, he wrote, came from "nature's gift of three vast bodies of water"—the Atlantic, the Pacific, and the Arctic—"interposed between this country and any other power that might constitute a serious menace to its safety." He went on to suggest that while "[a]nxieties about security have kept the growth of optimism within bounds among other peoples, . . . the relative absence of such anxieties in the past has helped, along with other factors, to make optimism a national philosophy in America."[1]

As Woodward developed it, this was anything but an optimistic view of American history. His own writings had shown that many Americans—on both sides of the racial divide—had never really been secure, whether as a result of slavery and the segregation that followed, or as a consequence of the Confederacy's defeat in the Civil War. He acknowledged that there had been periods, for all Americans, in which security had been problematic: the dangers of immigration in the first place, and of life on the frontier once there; the struggle for independence, secure borders, and maritime rights in the late eighteenth and early nineteenth centuries. Finally, Woodward was writing at a moment when the United States had become vulnerable, for the first time ever, to the possibility of a devastating attack on any portion of its territory. The Soviet Union had just acquired thermonuclear weapons and the intercontinental ballistic missiles with which to deliver them. Security could never again be taken for granted as easily as it once had been.

Still, Woodward insisted, the fact that Americans had not had to exhaust themselves in ensuring their own safety was a distinctive characteristic, shared with few other nations. It had helped to determine who we were. The American ideal—the reason so many people over so many years were willing to risk so much to *become* Americans—had been to insulate domestic life from a violent external world: to avoid the collisions between the personal and the historical that cause dates to be divorced, in our minds, from the years in which they occur. Vann Woodward's dark question, therefore, was this: what would it mean, for Americans, to have to live henceforth in a world of insecurity, in which this separation of the personal from the historical could no longer be assumed?

We were fortunate enough not to have to answer that question during the rest of the Cold War. The danger of nuclear attack never disappeared, but its probability diminished to such an extent that security came to reside, in the minds of many strategists, precisely in the fact that the United States and the Soviet Union did have thousands of missiles, armed with nuclear warheads, aimed at one another. Mutual vulnerability, indeed the capacity for mutual assured destruction, was thought to be an excellent thing.[2] Whether because or in spite of this bizarre standoff, the testing of the American character that Vann Woodward foresaw failed to materialize within his lifetime.

That's one of the reasons why the sight of smoke rising over New York and Washington on September 11, 2001, was such a shock: an attack had at last come, although at an unexpected time and in an even more unexpected way. The effect, though, was close to the one Woodward had anticipated. Suddenly Americans could no longer confidently work, travel, or even stay at home without fearing for their lives. The boundaries between everyday existence and a dangerous world had been shattered, as had the assumption of safety that had long since become, or so Woodward had argued, part of what it meant to be an American. September 11th was not just a national security crisis. It was a national identity crisis as well.

It was not the first time, however, that the smoke from a surprise attack had risen over the national capital. Most Americans have forgotten what little they may have learned in school about the War of 1812, and as a result another date—August 24, 1814—has no particular meaning for them. It should, because that was the day a British army marched into the newly established city of Washington, having routed its ragged defenders, and proceeded to burn the Capitol and the White House.[3] There's an eerie connection between these events and those of September 11, 2001, for it's likely that the intended target of United Flight 93, which crashed in Pennsylvania after the passengers overwhelmed the hijackers, was one of those two buildings. History rarely repeats itself, but on this occasion it came damn close.

So why doesn't August 24th have a place in our memories similar to that of December 7th, or November 22nd, or now September 11th? It's partly, I think, because the casualties on both sides that day were relatively light, because the attack didn't lead to anything worse, and because it was quickly overshadowed by Andrew Jackson's decisive defeat of the British at the Battle of New Orleans early in 1815. Yet another reason is that the invasion came at the end of the war, not at its beginning: peace negotiations had been underway for several months, and on Christmas Eve, 1814, they produced the Treaty of Ghent, which acknowledged victory for neither side but simply restored the status quo. Jackson's victory, however satisfying, had been unnecessary—the word simply hadn't gotten there in time. So if anyone these days remembers the burning of Washington, what tends to come to mind is the comic-opera character of the event: the farcical defense of the city, President James Madison's ignominious departure from it, and of course the intrepid Dolley snatching George Washington's portrait off the White House wall as she made her own exit, thereby saving at least a national symbol, if not national dignity.

For Americans at the time, though, the humiliation was sharp. To sense how much so, consider the now thankfully never sung third verse of *The Star-Spangled Banner,* composed by Francis Scott Key to celebrate the failure of the British to take Fort McHenry in Baltimore harbor after their withdrawal from Washington:

> And where is that band who so hauntingly swore
> That the havoc of war and the battle's confusion
> A home and country, shall leave us no more?
> Their blood has washed out their foul foot step's pollution
> No refuge could save the hireling and slave
> From the terror of flight or the gloom of the grave.[4]

It was a song intended, rather in the spirit of Dolley Madison, to salvage something from a national embarrassment, and it ought to remind us that security and the self-confidence that comes with it have not always been part of the American experience.

"It would be difficult to overestimate the effect," historians James Chace and Caleb Carr have written of the attack on Washington in 1814. "[T]he threats from abroad that had so long perplexed American leaders had proved grimly real. Thus mindful of the dangers confronting their nation, Americans prepared to commit themselves to the *enlarged* task of providing for their own safety."[5] The word "enlarged" here is critical, for the pattern set by this now barely remembered violation of homeland security is one that has persisted ever since: that for the United States, *safety comes from enlarging, rather than from contracting, its sphere of responsibilities.*[6]

Most nations seek safety in the way most animals do: by withdrawing behind defenses, or making themselves inconspicuous, or otherwise avoiding whatever dangers there may be. Americans, in contrast, have generally responded to threats—and particularly to surprise attacks—by taking the offensive, by becoming more conspicuous, by confronting, neutralizing, and if possible overwhelming the sources of danger rather than fleeing from them. Expansion, we have assumed, is the path to security.

This was by no means a new idea in 1814. Benjamin Franklin had had something like it in mind as early as 1751 when he expressed confidence that a high birth rate would in time produce more Englishmen on his side of the ocean than on the other: the implication was that an island could not indefinitely rule a continent.[7] James Madison had argued, in the 10th *Federalist,* that growth would ensure the safety of republicanism—a form of government previously not thought possible in a large territory—by generating the contending interests necessary to balance one another.[8] Thomas Jefferson surely had security through expansion in mind when he overcame his strict constructionist principles and jumped at the opportunity to purchase the Louisiana Territory from France in 1803, instantaneously doubling the size of the United States.[9]

Prior to the War of 1812, however, there was no long-term strategy linking security to expansion. Even as he was acquiring Louisiana, Jefferson was reducing the size of the army and navy while maintaining a policy of neutrality toward Great Britain and France. When the Napoleonic Wars began to endanger American maritime rights, he had little choice but to respond—through the Embargo Act—by contracting American interests. The United States would refuse to trade, lest it be forced to defend its right to trade. The effects, though, were so humiliating that by the end of 1811 the mood in Congress had turned around, insisting on the defense of *all* interests including reputation, despite the fact that neither that body nor the recently installed Madison administration had done much more than Jefferson to provide the means of accomplishing such a task.[10] With foreign policy oscillating between appeasement and belligerence, with such glaring gaps between proclaimed ends and available means, it's hardly surprising that the United States stumbled into an unnecessary war, that the war itself was so badly managed, or that, once peace had returned, Americans began to take the requirements of national security and grand strategy more seriously.

For if the British could occupy and burn Washington almost as an afterthought while winding up a war against France that had lasted for almost a quarter of a century, what did that imply about American vulnerability once the fighting in Europe had ended? To the continental monarchies that had vanquished Napoleon, the historian George Dangerfield has emphasized, the United States was "little more than a grimy republican thumbprint" upon the pages of history.[11] Great Britain was only slightly more sympathetic: it had grudgingly reconciled itself to American independence, but its naval superiority gave it the means of challenging that independence again if it should ever choose to do so. Jefferson's prewar preference for *hiding*—for securing interests by contracting them—clearly would not work in a postwar world in which dangers had not diminished. A new approach was badly needed.

The man who devised it was John Quincy Adams, the most influential American grand strategist of the nineteenth century. The son of the second president of the United States and already the nation's most experienced diplomat, Adams had helped to negotiate the Treaty of Ghent and in 1817 became Secretary of State under President James Monroe. His accomplishments in this position far outweighed those of his own subsequent one-term presidency. For it was Adams, more than anyone else, who worked out the methods by which expansion could be made to provide the security that C. Vann Woodward, over a century later, would write about. These sound surprisingly relevant in the aftermath of September 11th: they were preemption, unilateralism, and hegemony.[12]

▲ ▼

First, *preemption*. Adams was keenly aware of the fact that the United States had vast borders to defend, but only limited means with which to defend them. It would never be able to anticipate all of the possible places, times, and ways by which another attack might come; and as the nation grew in territory and population the problem could only get worse. There was still a European presence to worry about, for although France had relinquished its last continental possession with the sale of Louisiana, Great Britain retained Canada and claimed the Oregon Territory, Russia retained Alaska and claimed the Pacific Coast almost as far south as San Francisco, and Spain—however tenuously—still controlled Florida, Mexico, Central America, and much of South America. There were, as well, what we would today call "non-state actors"—native Americans, pirates, marauders, and other free agents—ready to raid lightly defended positions along an advancing frontier. The first problem for a strategy of seeking security through expansion, therefore, was how to keep that expansion itself from generating new sources of insecurity.

Adams found an answer in Spanish Florida. Acting with ques-
tionable authorization from the Monroe administration, Jackson
had invaded that territory in 1818 after a series of attacks across
the border by Creeks, Seminoles, and escaped slaves. He also exe-
cuted two Englishmen whom he suspected of having organized
the raids, thereby creating a potentially dangerous diplomatic inci-
dent, not just with Spain but also Great Britain. Adams alone came
to Jackson's defense, persuading the rest of Monroe's cabinet that
the United States ought not to apologize for what had happened
but rather take advantage of it by claiming the right to act preemptively in such situations. The interests of the United States could
"as little compound with impotence as with perfidy," he instructed
the Spanish, in one of his most formidable diplomatic notes. Spain
must either garrison Florida with sufficient forces to prevent future
incursions, or it must "cede to the United States a province . . .
which is in fact a derelict, open to the occupancy of every en-
emy, civilized or savage, of the United States, and serving no other
earthly purpose than as a post of annoyance to them."[13]

The modern term "failed state" did not appear in Adams's
note, but he surely had that idea in mind when he insisted that
power vacuums were dangerous and that the United States should
therefore fill them. "I . . . gave [my opinion]," he had written of a
similar case a year earlier, "that the marauding parties . . . ought to

be broken up immediately."[14] One could no more entrust one's security to the cooperation of enfeebled neighboring states than to the restraint of agents controlled, as a result, by no state.

If that principle made sense in dealing with Spanish Florida, though, why would it not also make sense in countering the threats posed by native Americans along the entire line of western settlement? The dangers to life and property were no less severe, and as Jackson himself asked pointedly after entering the White House in 1829, who would "prefer a country covered with forests and ranged by a few thousand savages" to one "occupied by more than 12,000,000 happy people, and filled with all the blessings of liberty, civilization, and religion?"[15] Adams came in time to regret the brutal relocations of "savages" that Jackson carried out,[16] but Jackson's argument—that an expanding "civilization" spread out along an insecure frontier had the right of preemption—was a predictable extension of Adams's own thinking, as well as a powerful justification for such dispossessions throughout the rest of the nineteenth century.[17]

The doctrine of preemption also came, in time, to justify expansion at the expense of states that *might* fail. The administration of James K. Polk cited, among its reasons for annexing Texas in 1845, concerns that that territory might not be able to retain the independence it had won from the Mexicans nine years earlier, and that the British or the French might then take it over. Similar hypotheticals caused Polk to welcome—some historians say to provoke—the war with Mexico that soon followed, since it brought the opportunity to take California, whose great harbors at San Diego, Monterey, and San Francisco might also be vulnerable to seizure by Europeans.[18] The taking of California, in turn, required the extension of American sovereignty over all the territory—present-day Arizona, New Mexico, Colorado, Utah, and Nevada—that lay in between. Now even the prospect of power vacuums invited preemption.

These actions too stretched the "derelict" state argument beyond where Adams wanted to take it. By the end of his life he had come to see that whatever continental expansion might do for national security, it could well undermine domestic tranquility by bringing new slave states into the union and thus upsetting the delicate balance that had, so far, prevented civil war.[19] Nevertheless, the reasoning Polk used to defend such expansion—that an independent Texas or a thinly populated California might *eventually* be seized by hostile Europeans, thereby endangering American security—surely echoed that of Adams when he justified Jackson's invasion of Spanish Florida in 1818.[20]

Nor did preemption disappear with the completion of continental expansion. Consider what happened after what appeared to be another surprise attack, the sinking of the *U.S.S. Maine* in Havana harbor on February 15, 1898. It's not even clear now that this was an attack: there's evidence pointing to an internal explosion, perhaps of the ship's coal bunker.[21] At the time, though, Spain, which still ruled Cuba, got the blame, and two months later the United States declared war. Plans were already in place for a preemptive attack on the Spanish fleet at Manila—the Philippines being one of the few other Spanish colonies at the time—and on May 1, 1898, Commodore George Dewey carried out that action with great success. President William McKinley then followed this act of military preemption with a far more sweeping political one: his decision to take all of the Philippines, not because the United States had any clear idea of what to do with them or what benefits it would derive from having seized them, but rather out of the fear that the crumbling of Spanish authority there would allow other more powerful states—in this case Germany or Japan—to take them over.[22]

Over the next two decades, Theodore Roosevelt, William Howard Taft, and Woodrow Wilson would use similar arguments to justify a succession of preemptive interventions in Venezuela, the Dominican Republic, Haiti, Nicaragua, and ultimately Mexico, on the grounds that instability within those countries might give the European great powers—especially Germany—grounds for intervening. As Roosevelt put it in 1904, "[c]hronic wrongdoing, or an impotence which results in a general loosening of the ties of civilized society, may . . . ultimately require intervention by some civilized nation, and in the Western Hemisphere . . . may force the United States, however reluctantly, . . . to the exercise of an international police power."[23]

The United States therefore assumed the responsibility for maintaining order, collecting revenues, and paying off debts wherever indigenous regimes in the Caribbean or Central America were unable to do so. The Platt Amendment, written into Cuba's constitution by the Americans in 1901, reserved the right to intervene in that state's internal affairs at any time Washington deemed it advisable. The Panamanian revolution of 1903 and the subsequent construction of the canal across the isthmus were themselves acts of preemption, orchestrated by Roosevelt, with a view to keeping anyone else from building so strategic a waterway in so sensitive a spot. And Wilson's protracted military interventions in Mexico began in 1914 in an effort to prevent the Germans—who were rumored to be shipping machine guns—from exploiting domestic instability there.[24]

Concerns about "failed" or "derelict" states, then, are nothing new in the history of United States foreign relations, nor are strategies of preemption in dealing with them. So when President

George W. Bush warned, at West Point in June 2002, that Americans must "be ready for preemptive action when necessary to defend our liberty and to defend our lives," he was echoing an old tradition rather than establishing a new one.[25] Adams, Jackson, Polk, McKinley, Roosevelt, Taft, and Wilson would all have understood it perfectly well.

Equally influential within the American diplomatic tradition was a second Adams doctrine, that of *unilateralism*. The idea here was that the United States could not rely upon the goodwill of others to secure its safety, and therefore should be prepared to act on its own. George Washington famously expressed this view in his Farewell Address of 1796 when—reacting against complications that had arisen from the Franco-American alliance of 1778—he advised against such permanent relationships in peacetime. What's not as widely known, however, is that Washington may have gotten the idea from some of John Quincy Adams's earliest writings as a young man: "[R]eal independence," he had insisted in 1793, in an essay Washington read, required a disconnection "from all European interests and European politics."[26]

This aversion to entanglement was by no means an objection to treaties. Adams was proud of his role in negotiating the one with

Great Britain that ended the War of 1812, as well as the 1818 treaty, also with Britain, that established the Canadian boundary. His crowning achievement was the Transcontinental Treaty of 1819, in which he bullied Spain into not only relinquishing Florida but also accepting a northern boundary for its Mexican territories drawn all the way to the Pacific—this at a time when the United States itself possessed no clear title to land beyond the Rocky Mountains.[27] Alliances, though, were something else again. Americans, Adams argued, should accept no binding obligation to align their long-term interests with those of any other state, or to pledge mutual assistance when those interests were challenged. Nor should the United States *overtly* cooperate, even in the absence of a formal alliance, even with a state whose interests paralleled its own.

Adams's unilateralism became clear when Spanish authority collapsed throughout most of Latin America—the only exceptions were Cuba and Puerto Rico—in the early 1820s. It was not at all certain that the newly independent republics to the south would be able to retain their sovereignty, and there was even talk that France, Austria, and Russia might help Spain restore it, or perhaps attempt to assume it themselves. The British, alarmed by this prospect, had suggested a joint Anglo-American statement ruling out future European colonization in the western hemisphere, an idea that attracted the interest not just of President Monroe but also of former presidents Jefferson and Madison.[28] Adams transformed the British proposal into a unilateral pronouncement, however, despite the fact that the United States had no means whatever of enforcing such a policy. He had shrewdly calculated that Great Britain, with its navy, did have such means, and that its own interests in this instance would complement those of the United States even in the absence of a formal commitment. It was more dignified, Adams memorably said, "to avow our principles explicitly," rather than "to come in as a cock-boat in the wake of the British man-of-war."[29]

Herein lay the basis—in Washington's Farewell Address and in the Monroe Doctrine—for what would later become known as isolationism, a persistent theme in the history of American foreign policy. The term is a misnomer, for the United States never actually attempted to *isolate* itself from the rest of the world, as did Japan did from the seventeenth to the nineteenth century. Americans were always extensively involved in international trade, and a steady flow of immigration, together with improvements in transportation and communications, produced a complex web of international cultural connections as well.[30] The United States did, however, avoid commitments to act in concert with other great powers against future contingencies which no one could foresee. The 1778 alliance with France, finally terminated by mutual consent in 1800, had shown the dangers that could arise from such obligations. The Monroe Doctrine provided a blueprint for how interests could be advanced henceforth without such risks.

This unilateralist approach to the world survived for well over a century, even after the United States had made the shift from regional to global power. The long-delayed *rapprochement* with Britain at the end of the nineteenth century produced no formal alliance. Secretary of State John Hay's Open Door policy in China echoed the Monroe Doctrine in its attempt—much less successful, as it turned out—to exploit interests that paralleled those of other countries without assuming American commitments. The United States intervened decisively in World War I but only as an "associated," not an "allied," power; and when President Wilson proposed a peace to be enforced by a League of Nations obligated to act against future wars, his own country repudiated it. Unilateralism reached its apex during the 1920s and 1930s when, despite the power the United States now had to shape the course of events throughout the world, Americans refused to use that power lest it somehow compromise their own so highly prized freedom of action.

Even more persistently than preemption, then, the unilateralist view of American interests that Adams defined shaped the manner in which the United States conducted its relations with the rest

of the world right up to the outbreak of World War II. So in this respect also the evidence of a unilateralist "turn" in post-Cold War
American foreign policy—apparent in the Clinton administration,
but far more pronounced in that of George W. Bush[31]—reflects a return to an old position, not the emergence of a new one.

Finally, *hegemony*. As an experienced observer of the European
balance of power system, John Quincy Adams emphatically rejected any idea that the United States could or should co-exist, on
equal terms, with any other great power on the North American
continent. The choice, he wrote as early as 1811, was between, on
the one hand, having "an endless multitude of little insignificant
clans and tribes at eternal war with one another for a rock, or a fish
pond, the sport and fable of European masters and oppressors,"
or, on the other, "a nation, coextensive with the North American
continent, destined by God and nature to be the most populous
and most powerful people ever combined under one social com-
pact."[32]

Given the fact that most of the new world was still under European control, a balance of power could reasonably have been expected to emerge there, much as it had in the old world. It was Adams, fearing eternal wars over rocks and fish ponds, who made it a

goal of American strategy to keep that from happening. His doing so was all the more remarkable given the weakness of American military and naval capabilities at the time. What he saw,
though, was that time was on the side of the United States: that
the nation's population, economy, and potential strength could
only grow, while the ability of the European powers to control ad-
joining territories could only diminish. There was no reason, hence,
to hide hegemonic aspirations: "any effort on our part to reason
the world out of a belief that we are ambitious will have no other
effect than to convince them that we add to our ambition hypocrisy."[33]

There were, to be sure, limits to this vision of continental hegemony. The United States could not attempt again to invade Canada—as it had tried unsuccessfully to do during the War of 1812—
without risking war again with Great Britain and thus seeing American seaports and maritime commerce become hostage to the superiority of the British navy. Conversely, however, Britain could not
risk war with the United States without the prospect of seeing Canada, with its long undefended land border, held hostage to American armies. What resulted, over time, was a compromise: Britain
would not challenge the hegemonic aspirations of the United
States to the south and west, in return for which the United States
would accept a continued British presence in the north.[34]

The other limit had to do with racism. Even those expansion-ists who welcomed the addition of slave states to the Union as a result of the annexation of Texas and the war with Mexico did so on the grounds that a considerable number of Americans had already emigrated to the territories in question. They drew the line at the prospect of taking other territories—what was left of Mexico, for ex-ample, or Spain's remaining colonies in Cuba and Puerto Rico—where the assimilation of predominantly non-white populations would be required.[35] It would not be crossed until 1898, when the United States annexed the independent state of Hawaii and took Puerto Rico and the Philippines—but still not Cuba—from Spain during the Spanish-American War. The Filipino insurrection that quickly followed led many Americans to regard the acquisition of an overseas empire as having been a mistake, however, and the experiment was not repeated.[36]

The solution to this problem of limits, ultimately, was to make a distinction between sovereignty and spheres of influence. Ameri-can security could not require the expansion of sovereignty ev-erywhere, because that would change the character of American society itself, thereby risking what hegemony was supposed to safeguard. It was again Adams who best stated the principle: the United States "goes not abroad, in search of monsters to destroy," he insisted in his great 4th of July address in 1821. Were it otherwise, "she might become the dictatress of the world," but "she would be no longer the ruler of her own spirit."[37]

Security could best be assured, instead, by making certain that no other great power gained sovereignty within geographic proximity of the United States. The fact that small powers dominated regions to the south was thought not to be a threat as long as Europeans refrained from exploiting their weakness. A secessionist American republic would be a threat, though: hence the immense expenditure in money and lives the Union was willing to make to defeat the Confederacy. Even so, Americans on both sides of the Civil War could agree, within months of its end, on the importance of ousting the Emperor Maximilian from Mexico, he having been installed there while that conflict was going on by France's Napoleon III.[38] For the next century, the United States would be quick to rebuff all subsequent efforts by other great powers to establish footholds of any kind, not just in North America, but throughout the western hemisphere. With the single exception of Cuba during the Cold War, it succeeded.[39]

"Today," Secretary of State Richard Olney proclaimed in 1895, "the United States is practically sovereign on this continent. . . . [I]ts infinite resources combined with its isolated position render it master of the situation and practically invulnerable as against any or all other powers."[40] It was a brash restatement of Adams's contempt for cloaking ambition with hypocrisy, made with a view to reminding the British that there was no balance of power in North and South America: there was, instead, a preponderance of power in the hands of the United States. Lord Salisbury's government did not dispute the point, thereby confirming as a reality at the end of the nineteenth century the vision of American hegemony Adams had articulated at its beginning.

And what of the twentieth century—and the twenty-first? Let me suggest here only that, for all of his concern about taking on monsters abroad, had John Quincy Adams lived to see the end of the Cold War, he would not have found the position of the United States within the international system an unfamiliar one. Despite the difference between a continental and a global scale, the American commitment to maintaining a preponderance of power[41]—as distinct from a balance of power—was much the same in the 1990s as it had been in his day. Nor would Adams have detected evidence of hypocrisy cloaking ambition in what President Bush announced at West Point in June 2002: that "America has, and intends to keep, military strengths beyond challenge."[42]

In responding to the second attack on Washington and all the other horrors that took place on September 11, 2001, therefore, the

Bush administration, whether intentionally or not, has been drawing upon a set of traditions that go back to the aftermath of the first
attack on Washington 187 years earlier. This is hardly surprising,
for if C. Vann Woodward was right in claiming that the benefits
of mostly free security shaped our character as a people and nur-
tured our development as a nation, then the methods that secured those benefits—in short, the grand strategy of John Quincy
Adams—should be embedded within our national consciousness.
They would be the default: when in doubt, fall back on these.[43]

If that's right, though, it raises an interesting question about
the American experience with security and surprise attack in the
twentieth century. For although the ideas of John Quincy Adams
and George W. Bush do appear to have paralleled one another following the first and second attacks on Washington, in 1814 and
2001, Franklin D. Roosevelt chose quite a different course in the aftermath of the other great surprise attack in American history, the
one that took place at Pearl Harbor on December 7, 1941. Why that
was the case—why our actions throughout World War II and the
Cold War differed so sharply from our earlier pattern of response to
danger, as well as from the one upon which we now seem to have
embarked—these are themes I'll take up in the next chapter.

I want to close this one, though, with the memory of another
famous Yale historian, Samuel Flagg Bemis, long since dead but

still the greatest authority on the foreign policy and grand strategy of John Quincy Adams. The occasion was a lecture at the University of Texas at Austin in the early 1960s, and I was there as a shy and silent undergraduate. Someone in the audience had the boldness to ask Professor Bemis whether the Mexican War had not resulted from an act of aggression on the part of the United States. "Yes," Bemis acknowledged with unexpected mildness, "it certainly had." Then he added, much more emphatically, with the sweep of an arm that seemed to encompass, not just the entire classroom, but the entire university, indeed the entire state: "But you wouldn't want to give it all back, would you?"

It's far more fashionable now than it was in Bemis's day to deplore the methods by which the United States came to dominate the North American continent. It did so at the expense of victims to whom today's university history courses—Yale's are no exception—devote considerably more attention than they do to the policies that generated that expansion, or to the benefits it provided. I suspect strongly, though, that most Americans today—and even Adams in his day, for all of his reservations about Jackson and Polk—would answer Bemis's question as he anticipated his Texas audience would: "No, we wouldn't want to give it all back."

All of which suggests a disconnection in our thinking between the security to which we've become accustomed and the means by which we obtained it. We've tended in recent years to condemn the methods even as we've continued to enjoy—and now seek to extend—the benefits. Can we have it both ways? Well, maybe: F. Scott Fitzgerald once wrote that the sign of a first-rate intelligence is the ability to hold two opposed ideas in one's mind at the same time. But the essays in which he made this observation were entitled, rather discouragingly, *The Crack-Up*.

The better approach, I think, is to acknowledge the moral ambiguity of our history. Like most other nations, we got to where we are by means that we cannot today, in their entirety, comfortably endorse. Comfort alone, however, cannot be the criterion by which a nation shapes its strategy and secures its safety. The means of confronting danger do not disqualify themselves from consideration solely on the basis of the uneasiness they produce. Before we too quickly condemn how our ancestors dealt with such problems, therefore, we might well ask ourselves two questions, both of which follow from the one I heard Bemis ask four decades ago: What would *we* have done had if we had been in their place then? And, even scarier, how comfortable will *our* descendants be with the choices we make today?

# 3

## THE TWENTIETH CENTURY

Not the least of the shocks associated with the events of September 11, 2001, were the similarities to another surprise attack that took place almost sixty years earlier: the Japanese strike against Pearl Harbor on December 7, 1941. Both were bolts from the blue on bright mornings. Both achieved total surprise, as the result of a total failure of intelligence. Both employed familiar technologies in unfamiliar ways: the Japanese by launching fighter-bombers from aircraft carriers; the terrorists by turning civilian airliners into cruise missiles. Both attacks took place on American territory, and both produced casualties in the thousands. Both led to immediate declarations of war. And both so burned themselves into the nation's consciousness—and indeed the consciousness of most of the rest of the world—that the days on which they occurred would no longer require, in memory, the specification of a year: both would remain, as Franklin D. Roosevelt said of the first, dates that would "live in infamy."

To be sure, there were differences. The Japanese attack was the deliberate act of a state that had long used military force to advance its interests. It came after an extended series of escalating crises, so that the outbreak of war was no surprise, only the manner in which it happened. None of these things was true of the terrorist attacks. Their perpetrators, so far as we know, acted without the authorization of any state. There had been a series of earlier bombings—the World Trade Center itself in 1993, the Khobar Tower barracks in Saudi Arabia in 1996, the embassies in Kenya and Tanzania in 1998, and the *U.S.S. Cole* in 2000—but the pattern that lay behind these became clear only after September 11th. There were also differences in the targets hit. However one may view the morality of a sneak attack conducted prior to a declaration of war, there's no question that Pearl Harbor was a military target. Maybe, by a generous stretching of the term, the Pentagon was too on September 11th. That can hardly have been the case, though, for the Twin Towers and the people who worked there. The attack on them was, and was no doubt intended to be, the mass killing of civilians who not only had had no hand in preparations for a war or in the conduct of it, but who were also for the most part unaware of the fact that a war was even going on.[1]

Finally, there was a difference in the kinds of wars Presidents Roosevelt and Bush declared in the wake of December 7th and September 11th. Roosevelt demanded, and got, the instant mobilization of the country: for the next four years, all Americans would live lives dramatically different from what they'd been before. Bush requested, and only partially received, what amounted to a global police action against terrorism, combined with a call for vigilance at home and abroad, combined with the suggestion that, despite what had happened, Americans should carry on with their ordinary lives. Whereas Roosevelt had insisted that a return to normality would hand victory to the nation's enemies, Bush took the view that a departure from normality would do the same.[2]

And what about the effects of December 7, 1941, on the subsequent evolution of American grand strategy? I argued in the previous chapter that surprise attacks tend to sweep away old conceptions of national security and what it takes to achieve it. They bring about new—and sometimes radically different—assessments of vital interests and available capabilities. I suggested as well that there's a pattern in the way Americans have gone about this: that when confronted with unexpected dangers, we tend to expand rather than contract our sphere of responsibilities. Running and hiding has rarely been our habit.

Thus, over the decade that followed the first surprise attack on United States soil—the occupation of Washington by the British in August 1814, and the subsequent burning of the Capitol and the White House—American leaders evolved a strategy of forestalling future challenges by enlarging American interests. The principal elements of that strategy were: preemption where marauders might exploit the weakness of neighboring states, or where that weakness might tempt stronger states to establish a presence; unilateralism, so that the United States need not rely upon any other state to guarantee its security; and, finally, hegemony over the North American continent, in order that the dominant international system there would reflect a preponderance of American power rather than a balance among several powers, with all the possibilities for wars, commercial rivalries, and revolutions that the latter arrangement had led to in Europe.

Given that history and the psychology it produced, it's hardly surprising that these preferences for preemption, unilateralism, and hegemony resurfaced in the aftermath of September 11th as American leaders scrambled to regain the security the nation seemed to have lost: deep roots do not easily disappear. Despite some obvious differences in personality, John Quincy Adams and George W. Bush would not have had much difficulty, on matters of national security, in understanding one another.

Despite some similarities in personality, however, Franklin D. Roosevelt and George W. Bush might well have had such difficulties. For although the American sphere of responsibility also expanded dramatically in the aftermath of the surprise attack at Pearl Harbor, it did so without relying on preemption, unilateralism, or at least the *overt* seeking of hegemony. Since Roosevelt was, historians are coming to realize, the most influential American grand strategist of the twentieth century, it's worth looking more closely at his reasons for rejecting these long-established nineteenth-century practices. They would largely shape the American conduct, not just of World War II, but of the Cold War as well.[3]

The best place to begin is with a problem American leaders had been worrying about for at least half a century prior to 1941, but had failed to resolve: how far did the American sphere of responsibility have to extend in order to ensure American security? The answer had been clear enough when the only potential challengers were European, when the only means available to project military power across great distances were sailing ships, and when the nation with the largest number of these—Great Britain—itself sympathized with the American objective of keeping the western hemisphere off limits to future colonization. It sufficed, under these circumstances, for the United States to dominate the North American continent. By the beginning of the twentieth century, however, that situation had changed. The principal reason was a transportation revolution that had diminished the Americans' most important strategic asset: their geographical separation from everyone else who might threaten them.

The military forces available to Napoleon, Nelson, or even to Andrew Jackson moved little faster than those commanded by Hannibal and Caesar two thousand years earlier. But by the time of the Crimean War in the early 1850s, it had become possible to use steam as well as wind to propel naval vessels, thereby greatly enhancing their speed and maneuverability. By the American Civil War a decade later, armies were traveling by rail, with similarly striking effects on the conduct of land warfare. And in 1903, shortly after the conclusion of the Spanish-American War, a couple of imaginative bicycle mechanics from Dayton, Ohio, attached wings to an internal combustion engine, making possible the conduct of war from the air as well as from land and sea. A central premise of the Adams strategy had been that distance itself was a means of defense. But now distance was being conquered.

What's surprising is not that these technological innovations produced a revolution in American thinking about national security, but rather that it took so long for this to occur. It was clear, well before the United States entered World War I, that the nature of warfare had radically changed. No consensus emerged on how to deal with these changes, though, until the United States entered World War II. The reason, I think, is that for all that happened in the decades preceding the Pearl Harbor attack, nothing shocked Americans sufficiently to meet what we might call the Dr. Samuel Johnson Test: "Depend on it, Sir," the great man once commented, "when a man knows he is to be hanged in a fortnight, it concentrates his mind wonderfully."[4] Despite a significantly altered strategic landscape, dangers before December 7, 1941, were not convincingly clear and present, with the predictable result that American minds failed to concentrate.

Did danger come, for example, from the possibility that a single hostile power might gain control of some important part of the world, and thereby threaten American security? Theodore Roosevelt thought so, and sought to keep that from happening through demonstrations of naval strength, together with adroit diplomacy aimed at tilting against challengers to the balance of power in Europe and Northeast Asia. Did danger come from the possibility that the United States might be frozen out of overseas markets, access to which could be vital, in an increasingly integrated global economy, to American prosperity? William Howard Taft believed it did, and shifted the priorities of American foreign policy from Roosevelt's balancing to the expansion of commercial opportunities within an equally expanded framework of international law. Did danger come from the denial of democracy, from the possibility that the American model might not after all be applicable in the rest of the world? Woodrow Wilson was convinced of this, setting aside Taft's emphasis on "dollar diplomacy" in favor of efforts to "teach" people elsewhere, as he once said of the Mexicans, to elect "good men."

All of these concerns came together in 1917 to produce a dramatic—but temporary—departure from past practices: Wilson's decision to intervene on the Allied side in World War I. He was, at once, worried about the European balance of power if Germany won, fearful of damage to the American economy if Great Britain and France lost, and optimistic about the opportunity the war presented to advance the cause of democracy throughout the world. The effect was decisive. The arrival of American forces tipped the balance on the western front in 1918 and led to Germany's collapse. And in Wilson's mind, at least, the issue of how far the American sphere of responsibility must extend to ensure American security had now been settled: it would extend everywhere.

Wilson's concept of a League of Nations implied a commitment, from all of its members and certainly from the United States, to act collectively to resist future aggression wherever in the world it took place. The war had shown that security was a seamless web: if it came apart anywhere, the fabric could unravel everywhere. The international community must therefore prevent such threats to peace from developing, and if necessary retaliate against whoever had broken the peace.[5]

It's a lot easier for a revolution to occur in the mind of a single leader, though, than for that leader to persuade others to think in similar ways. Wilson discovered this fact with respect to his own countrymen. Germany's defeat left no comparably credible source of danger on the horizon: despite the technological revolution in the weapons of warfare, the geopolitical situation seemed to have reverted to what it had been throughout most of the nineteenth century, with a benign Great Britain the only state capable of deploying military power across the distances that separated the United States from the rest of the world. Why get involved, therefore, in the complex and counter-productive rivalries of exasperating Europeans or Asians, since none of these seemed likely to affect American interests? The familiar feeling of what C. Vann Woodward called "free security"—the sense that Americans didn't have to work very hard to be safe—now vigorously reasserted itself.

The Senate therefore rejected Wilson's League, and the American people with equal firmness repudiated his call for enlarged international responsibilities.[6] Instead they contracted these to what they had been throughout most of the nineteenth century, excepting only efforts to benefit from the expanded trade and investment opportunities the war had left in its wake. The United States contented itself, once again, with hegemony in the western hemisphere, combined with unilateralism in its dealings with the other great powers, as well as with such rudimentary structures for governing the international system as those powers had been able—using Wilson's blueprint—to devise. The result had few precedents: a nation that had accumulated and still retained enormous strength, both in material and moral terms, declined for the most part to use it.

And what of preemption, the third component of United States grand strategy in the nineteenth century? Apart from the taking of the Philippines in 1898, that doctrine had always applied to potential threats within the western hemisphere. There were few after World War I, and as a result Latin American policy, during the 1920s, shifted away from the use of force.[7] The first clear challenge to security elsewhere came only in 1931 with the Japanese invasion of Manchuria, a region that hardly seemed vital to the defense of the United States. And even if it had been, the onset of the Great Depression would have constrained whatever inclination there might have been to act: the discovery that going to war could restore prosperity would have to wait for another decade.[8]

The American reaction was much the same when Mussolini invaded Ethiopia in 1935, and when the newly rearmed government of Hitler in Germany reoccupied the Rhineland in 1936. Franklin D. Roosevelt, who worried about these developments, nevertheless found himself under increasing constraints from the United States Congress, which in the Neutrality Acts of 1935–37 mandated impartiality toward both aggressors and the victims of aggression when wars broke out. Even without these legislative impediments, FDR would have found any preemption of European aggressors difficult because their ultimate targets, the European democracies, seemed so determined to appease them.[9]

Still, the extent of American passivity was striking in this decade when dangers were growing rapidly in both Europe and Asia and when progress in naval and air technology was shrinking the space that separated them from the United States. Despite Roosevelt's efforts to counter this trend, the nation came closer during the late 1930s to *hiding* in the face of threats than it had done at any point since the years preceding the War of 1812, when the Jefferson and Madison administrations had also tried, with growing desperation, to maintain neutrality in an expanding European war. FDR himself, no slouch when it came to history, noted the parallel in an address to Congress in September 1939: this earlier attempt to hide, he reminded his audience, had been "a disastrous failure," having produced not just involvement in war—the opposite of what was intended—but also "the burning in 1814 of part of the Capitol in which we are assembled today."[10]

▲ ▼

It would take two more years and a far more devastating surprise attack to dispel the illusion that nineteenth-century strategies could ensure the nation's security in a twentieth-century world of diminished distances and therefore enhanced vulnerabilities; but by the time Americans sat down to their Sunday dinners on the evening of December 7, 1941, that point had been settled once and for all. It was clear in this case instantly, as it had become clear much more gradually after August 1814, that the United States had underestimated the dangers it faced, and that its sphere of responsibility would, as a consequence, significantly expand. The chief architect of that expansion—easily as influential in his own time as John Quincy Adams had been in his—was Franklin D. Roosevelt.

FDR's skills as a strategist have not always been appreciated. His own subordinates, frustrated by the devious and improvisational manner in which he wove his way through the complexities of domestic politics and great power diplomacy, found his methods baffling, even alarming.[11] Historians have charged him, at one time or another, with having dithered until it was too late in confronting the aggressors, with having then blundered into war with both Germany and Japan at the same time, with having then— against the advice of his closest ally, Winston Churchill—let military considerations and not geopolitical interests determine its conduct, and with having then been so naïve about his most powerful wartime ally, Stalin, that he failed to anticipate the Cold War that was bound to follow, thereby consigning half of Europe to half a century of Soviet domination.[12]

But historical reputations, like empires, rise and fall. It's clear now that FDR had never believed that Americans could remain secure in an international system that rewarded aggression while lacking the means of preventing war. He was, in this sense, a Wilsonian, fully inclined to accept, as a principle, the seamless web metaphor for international security. He was also, however, a far more skillful leader than Wilson, for he never neglected, as Wilson did, the need to keep *proclaimed* interests from extending beyond *actual* capabilities. This was the great consistency that explained FDR's inconsistencies. It helps to account for the fact that his strategy brought two separate wars to almost simultaneous conclusions with the victor far stronger than at their beginnings. It helps to explain why most scholars today have come around to the view that the presciently provocative British historian A. J. P. Taylor buried in a footnote in 1965: "Of the three great men at the top,

Roosevelt was the only one who knew what he was doing: he made the United States the greatest power in the world at virtually no cost."[13]

Taylor was of course exaggerating: there were costs for the Americans, in both lives and treasure, during World War II. He was right, though, to make the point that these were far less than those sustained by each of the other major combatants. As a consequence, the United States was able to move in a remarkably short period of time from a strategy that had limited itself to controlling the western hemisphere to one aimed at winning a global war and managing the peace that would follow. Equally significant is the fact that Roosevelt pulled off this expanded hegemony by scrapping rather than embracing the two other key components of Adams's strategy, unilateralism and preemption.

Adams and all subsequent shapers of United States foreign policy until Roosevelt had rejected *explicit* cooperation with other great powers to achieve American interests. They so valued freedom of action that they were prepared to forgo the benefits traditional diplomacy has always found in formal alliances—despite the fact that it had been just such an alliance, with France in 1778, that had secured American independence in the first place. Thus, even though the United States relied upon the strength of the British navy to enforce the Monroe Doctrine, it never acknowledged that it was doing so. The emergence of common adversaries failed to alter this pattern: hence Wilson's insistence on the United States being an "associated" but not an "allied" power in World War I.

And yet, even before Pearl Harbor, Roosevelt was well on the way to dismantling this unilateralist tradition. It was not just Great Britain's defense that was now vital to American security, he convinced the Congress and the country in securing support for the Lend-Lease Act of 1941; so too, after the German invasion that began in June, was the survival of the Soviet Union itself. This was an astonishing reversal for a country that, only half a decade earlier, had revived the Jeffersonian precedent of neutrality in the face of an impending European war. Three weeks after Pearl Harbor, Roosevelt made it official: there was not just an alliance linking the United States, Great Britain, and the Soviet Union, but a Grand Alliance. It in turn was to fight for the principles of a much broader organization that was as yet only a gleam in the president's eye: the United Nations.

So what had happened to American unilateralism? First, the Dr. Johnson Test had been met: there were now clear and present dangers across *both* of the oceans upon which the United States had traditionally relied for its security, but could no longer. Second, there had never been the possibility of *moral* neutrality with respect to German or Japanese aggression, despite an eroding but

persistent *legal* neutrality. The results of the 1938 Munich Conference were making the risks of appeasement painfully clear, not just
in Europe but in Asia as well.[14] Finally, the United States had been
attacked, literally by the Japanese on December 7th, figuratively—
and very foolishly—by Hitler when he declared war on the United
States four days later. Rearmament, by this time, was well underway: indeed Roosevelt had already committed the country to building an air force second to none to be equipped, if the technology
proved feasible, with atomic weapons.[15] These capabilities would
take time to develop, however, and some—like the bomb—might
never reach that stage. It was imperative, in the meantime, to ensure that adversaries did not prevail. Alliances were the only way to
do that.

There was another more subtle reason, however, why unilateralism would no longer work: Roosevelt intended for allies, at least
in Europe, to do most of the fighting. This idea had been implicit
in his "arsenal of democracy" concept prior to Pearl Harbor: the
United States would furnish weapons, but the British and the
Russians would actually use them. What's often not recognized,
though, is the extent to which FDR retained that objective after
American entry into the war. There was no way now to avoid send-
ing Americans into combat, but there was a way to keep casualties
to a minimum, thereby avoiding the mass slaughter that had made

World War I a defeat for all its European participants. It was to depend upon allies while simultaneously coming to their rescue.

A final problem with unilateralism had to do with the peace settlement that was to follow the war. The Grand Alliance had arisen out of necessity, not affinity. For all their personal camaraderie, Roosevelt and Churchill had different visions of the postwar world, especially when it came to the openness of markets and the future of empires. Those differences paled, however, alongside the ones that existed with the Soviet Union. Stalin's dictatorship was at least as autocratic as that of Hitler, and its record of murdering its own citizens was even worse. It clearly did not seek a world safe for democracy, capitalism, or much of anything else apart from its own immediate interests. Yet Roosevelt's strategy required keeping the Soviet Union in the war, because for every American who was dying while fighting it, some 60 Russians were doing so. How, then, to align American interests with the Red Army's capabilities?

FDR's answer was to embed conflicting unilateral priorities within a cooperative multilateral framework. The pursuit of national interests, he argued, need not preclude the emergence of collective interests, because nobody had an interest in fighting another great war. If, therefore, the present war could provide the incentive to build structures and procedures that would prevent new ones, then all would benefit. That was the key to Roosevelt's wartime diplomacy, which was as much a part of his grand strategy as was the deployment of military forces. And yet, with the single instructive example of Wilson's failure, it was a diplomacy very much at odds with anything the United States had attempted before.

For it was not just the American sphere of responsibility that was being expanded now. There was also implicit, in Roosevelt's idea of multilateralism, a rejection of what Americans had always thought about the rest of the world. The Adams strategy had assumed our own exceptionalism: other nations were not and would never be like us. The American task, Adams had insisted, was not to reform the world, but to rather to see that we were safe within it. Wilson had seen broader possibilities: that if democracy and capitalism spread throughout the world, security could become automatic. But he had allowed this interest to exceed the limits of what the United States could accomplish abroad and what Americans would accept at home. Roosevelt now revived the Wilsonian project, taking care though to couple it to a cold-blooded, at times even brutal, calculation of who had power and how they might use it.

He began, in 1942, with something resembling the old Quadruple Alliance against Napoleon: his proposal that "Four Policemen"—the United States, Great Britain, the Soviet Union, and Chiang Kai-shek's China—would simply run the postwar world,

bombing anyone else who would not go along. Roosevelt understood, though, that democracies could not indefinitely function in
this way. He therefore linked this realist vision to his own restatement of Wilsonian ideals, first articulated as the Four Freedoms
and the Atlantic Charter, then institutionalized as the United Nations. He subsequently added an equally important set of economic underpinnings in the form of the Bretton Woods system,
knowing from the experience of the 1930s what could happen to international cooperation if a global depression should return.

FDR quietly sought to ensure, in all of these structures, predominance for the United States: the purpose of including Nation-
alist China as one of the Four Policemen had been to give Washington a surrogate vote within that group; the purpose of a Security
Council veto in the United Nations was to make sure that that body
never acted against American interests; the purpose of Bretton
Woods was to perpetuate the economic hegemony with which the
United States was certain to end the war.

And why should allies agree to such self-serving arrange-
ments? Because, in their absence, there was sure to be something
worse, whether in the form of a less than decisive victory against
Germany and Japan, or a postwar economic collapse, or even a re-
play of the post World War I retreat by the United States back into
the unilateralism of the nineteenth century that had, in the eyes of

many more people than just Americans, contributed to the coming of World War II. American hegemony as FDR conceived it was now to be global, but in contrast to anything John Quincy Adams could ever have imagined, *it was to arise by consent.*

So what about preemption? What happened to the old idea that the United States, when confronting potential threats, had the right to remove them? To begin with, preemption makes little sense in the aftermath of a surprise attack because the target has already been preempted. Recovery takes a while, and even after it's occurred, preemption is pointless because the threat is now actual, not potential, and it's assumed on both sides that each will do whatever is necessary to prevail. The battle of Midway, for example, in which the United States Navy exploited an intelligence breakthrough to anticipate the location of the Japanese fleet, wasn't really preemption. It was more like the nautical equivalent of an ambush in a conflict already underway. Preemption generally applies to the next probable adversary—hence Adams's defense of Jackson's invasion of Spanish Florida in 1818—rather than to the one—the British in 1814—responsible for the surprise in the first place.

Preemption was an option for the United States in World War

II, however, because in the latter months of that conflict a next probable adversary was becoming visible on the horizon. Despite Roosevelt's best efforts to lock him into a mutually acceptable postwar settlement, Stalin had made it clear, by the time of FDR's death in April 1945, that he would not accept multilateralism: that he planned to impose a unilaterally controlled sphere of influence in eastern and central Europe, as he himself once put it, as far as his armies could reach.[16] This possibility had been apparent for some time, and it had led to talk of preemption, among the Americans and the British, in several ways: first, a plan to rush Anglo-American troops into as much of Germany as possible in the event of a sudden Nazi collapse, with a view to freezing the Russians out; second, Churchill's idea of shifting the second front from France to a location—he favored the Mediterranean—from which British and American forces might interpose themselves between the Red Army and the center of Europe; and third, when the German surrender was indeed imminent in the spring of 1945, Churchill's call for a quick thrust to take Berlin, rather than halting the British and American advance within previously agreed upon zones of occupation that would leave that city surrounded by Soviet controlled territory.[17]

The first of these options remained hypothetical because the Nazis did not suddenly collapse. Roosevelt rejected the other two, for reasons that remain controversial. Certainly there were military arguments against them and these carried the greatest weight: in line with their reluctance to take excessive casualties, both the president and his supreme commander in Europe, General Dwight D. Eisenhower, were not inclined to risk military operations for what Eisenhower said would be "purely political purposes."[18] But I suspect that Roosevelt had another consideration in mind as well: if there was to be a conflict with the Soviet Union, hot or cold, after the defeat of Nazi Germany, he did not want the United States to be seen as having started it. Roosevelt never said this explicitly. I'm deducing it from his actions, especially his reluctance to follow Churchill's advice and confront Stalin over his failure to keep the agreements he had made on Poland at the Yalta conference, as well as Stalin's allegations that the Americans had been negotiating for the secret surrender of German forces in Italy. Roosevelt had, however, explained a similar logic in the fall of 1941, when he had talked about "maneuvering" the Japanese into "firing the first shot."[19]

What he meant was that military action had to be linked to morality: to preempt even clear and present danger was to take the responsibility for *initiating* the use of force, and that always carries a cost. For Adams and Spanish Florida in 1818, it had been the risk that Spain might break off negotiations on a transcontinental boundary line, and that Great Britain might retaliate for the execution of its subjects at the hands of General Jackson. Through a combination of luck and skill, Adams averted these dangers. Polk in the Mexican War was not so fortunate. Preemption saddled him with charges, throughout the conflict, that he had started it: those grew into allegations of a slave state "conspiracy" that would ultimately fracture the Democratic and Whig parties and help bring about the Civil War. For McKinley in the Philippines, preemption left a legacy of uneasiness about distant colonial acquisitions that kept the United States from acquiring any more of them. In the end it was FDR himself who promised the Filipinos, in 1934, their eventual independence.

Why this discomfort with preemption, and why did it seem to grow as time went on? Perhaps it had to do with the standards to which Americans held themselves within their domestic legal system: attacking someone because you're convinced they're about to attack you, however psychologically satisfying, has never found much juridical justification. Perhaps it had to do with the behavior one expects from a nation that still regarded itself as different from most others: democracies didn't—or at least shouldn't—start wars. Perhaps it had to do, as the United States became more conscious of its role in the world, with the possibility that the world might in time follow the American example, which would have to appear to be above reproach. With respect to FDR and the coming confrontation with the Soviet Union, I think it had to do with all of these things and something else as well: his great *consistent* principle that proclaimed interests should not exceed actual capabilities.

For Roosevelt knew that with all the difficulties that had arisen, the Soviet Union in 1945 still commanded enormous good will, in both the United States and in much of Europe, because of the disproportionate burden it had borne in the war against Nazi Germany. To turn on that ally too abruptly could cause a backlash at home while making it harder to enlist allies in the cause abroad. The price of preemption would have been too great, even if it had been militarily feasible. If there was to be a postwar conflict with the Russians, FDR wanted them to "fire the first shot."

The history of American grand strategy during the Cold War is remarkable for the *infrequency* with which the United States acted unilaterally, as well as for top-level resistance to the idea of preemption and its related nuclear era concept, preventive war.[20] In this sense, post-World War II strategists rejected as thoroughly as had Roosevelt the Adams legacy that so strongly influenced American behavior toward the rest of the world throughout most of the nineteenth and the first four decades of the twentieth century. And yet, Adams would have had little to complain of when the end of the Cold War rolled around, for this repudiation of two of his great principles secured the third and most important one, which was hegemony: a preponderance of power—not a balance of power— and this time on a global scale. How did this happen?

Begin with the strategy of containment, the emergence of which, in 1946–47, marked the Truman administration's acknowledgment that FDR's hopes for cooperation with the Soviet Union had indeed failed.[21] What containment implied, figuratively if not literally, was the building of a wall: the world would be divided, with the Soviet Union contained behind the barrier thereby created. That still seemed to many at the time a preemptive approach, in which the *anticipation* of a conflict risked bringing it about. The Truman Doctrine speech of March 1947, with its blunt characterization of a world divided by "two ways of life," provoked criticism on just these grounds: however much one might object to what the Soviet Union was doing in eastern Europe, the president's rhetoric did give the appearance of firing the first shot.

The administration acted swiftly to repair the damage with the Marshall Plan: surely one of the most imaginative—and successful—grand strategic maneuvers in all of history. As outlined by Secretary of State George C. Marshall at Harvard in June of 1947, the proposal retained Roosevelt's idea of encompassing unilateral interests within a multilateral framework, for like the Bretton Woods system it appealed to an interest no one could openly oppose, which was postwar economic recovery. The Marshall Plan was, however, very much an act of Cold War strategy, designed to advance the interests of the United States and its western European allies. It was meant to divide Europe, on the grounds that it was better to save half of it than to see all of it succumb to the kind of desperation that might make it embrace the Soviet alternative.[22] The problem, in this case, was not how to get Stalin to fire the first shot, but *how to get him to build the wall* behind which he would then be contained.

It was another great American strategist, George F. Kennan, who came up with the answer, and it's one of which I suspect FDR would have approved: offer Marshall Plan aid to the Eastern Europeans and to the Soviet Union itself, with the expectation that Stalin would turn it down and that he would forbid the satellite states he controlled from accepting it either.[23] After a few days of nervousness for Kennan, this is indeed what happened. The Americans, from that moment on, occupied the moral high ground in Europe, and they never relinquished it. That's why it was possible to maintain a sphere of influence there—an expanded zone of responsibil-ity—with the consent of those who lived within it, a point demon-strated repeatedly by the free elections held throughout western Europe, only a few of which the newly formed Central Intelligence Agency felt it necessary to try to manipulate.[24] Such elections could never be held within the Soviet sphere of influence, because if they were, as Stalin, Khrushchev, and Brezhnev all knew, it would fall apart. As indeed it did when Gorbachev actually allowed them. Re-jecting preemption while embracing multilateralism, in this sense, served the United States—and its allies—very well.

A second case in which American officials followed a similar approach had to do with the atomic weapons FDR had decided to build before Pearl Harbor. The Americans possessed a monopoly over these devices from the time they tested their first one in the summer of 1945 until the Russians tested theirs in 1949; but be-cause of superior long-range bombing capabilities, the United States retained an effective monopoly well into the 1950s. So why did Washington not issue an ultimatum demanding the disman-tling of Soviet authority in eastern Europe, perhaps even of the So-viet dictatorship itself, backed up by the threat—to paraphrase Roosevelt on the Four Policemen—that Moscow would be bombed if it didn't go along? An odd pair of Englishmen, Winston Churchill and Bertrand Russell, called for just such a preventive war (it would have gone well beyond preemption) in 1948.[25] By the early 1950s there was renewed talk of such options within the Truman and Eisenhower administrations as they confronted the prospect of a military stalemate in the Korean War, and then again after the war as Eisenhower and his advisers considered the possibility that, with Soviet progress in developing thermonuclear weapons, American nuclear superiority might soon become a "wasting asset."

There was talk of preemption and even prevention—but never action. Historians have cited various reasons: during the late 1940s, concern over not having enough atomic bombs to knock the Soviet Union out of the war that would surely still result from their first use; in Korea, worries about finding appropriate targets; after that, concerns about what the environmental consequences of large-scale nuclear use might be; and through all of the above the moral burden of having introduced nuclear weapons into the conduct of war at Hiroshima and Nagasaki, a fact that set a high hurdle indeed against their future employment. Another important deterrent to initiating the use of nuclear weapons, however, was that this would be a unilateral act carried out by the leader of a multilateral coalition—the firing of a first and unimaginably destructive shot—and that the coalition itself might shatter as a result. De-

spite the irony, therefore, that the North Atlantic Treaty Organization came to rely upon nuclear first-use in the event of war, nuclear
first-use in the absence of war or its immediate prospect was never
seriously considered.[26]

Even at what most historians regard as the moment of maxi-
mum peril in the Cold War—when Soviet missiles in Cuba were
on the verge of becoming operational in October 1962—President
John F. Kennedy and his advisers considered but rejected preemption, very wisely since we now know that the Russians had both
strategic and tactical nuclear weapons on the island. That was not
known then, but what was known were the probable moral costs of
striking first. The United States would not, even under conditions
of clearest and most present danger, follow the Japanese example
at Pearl Harbor: indeed it's obvious from the tapes Kennedy se-
cretly made of his advisers' deliberations that simply invoking the
analogy was enough to sink the possibility that the United States
might emulate it.[27]

Fundamental to the American reluctance to preempt during
the Cold War, I think, was another principle that goes back to Roosevelt: that there should always be something worse than the
prospect of American domination. That might make little difference
in an arena in which hegemony was unchallenged, as was the case

for the United States in the western hemisphere throughout most of the nineteenth century. It made a huge difference, though, in an arena like the Cold War, where hegemony was contested and defections to the other side were always possible. Power is far easier to maintain, in such situations, when it's there by consent instead of coercion. The "something worse" principle ensures that that's the case.[28]

The influence of the United States therefore expanded during the postwar years, for the most part with the consent of those subject to it. The Soviet Union's influence also expanded, but without such consent. The explanation lay largely in the fact that American leaders held themselves accountable: they cared what the rest of the world thought, and tried to frame their policies accordingly. They sought, as much by instinct as by design, to apply the practices of domestic democratic statecraft internationally. Soviet leaders, in a manner consistent with their own domestic authoritarianism, attached much less importance to international accountability; and in those rare instances when they did attempt to achieve it, they did so much less skillfully than the Americans and their allies. The resulting *asymmetry of legitimacy*—the existence of two spheres of influence, one of which came across as "something worse" than the other one—did much to determine how the Cold War was fought and who would ultimately win it. The American rejection of unilateralism and preemption was, in turn, critical in bringing about that outcome.

▲ ▼

Franklin D. Roosevelt's legacy in responding to surprise attack, therefore, was very different from that of John Quincy Adams, despite the fact that the policies of both ultimately attained a preponderance of American power, Adams on a hemispheric scale and FDR on a global scale. The key distinction was this matter of consent. Adams didn't care whether anyone else welcomed the Monroe Doctrine: the point was to proclaim it, and let the compliant British worry about enforcing it. Allies, in his era, could only have impeded American freedom of action, thereby diminishing American security. The world would never resemble the United States; it was best, therefore, for the United States to stay aloof from the world. Roosevelt, however, cared a lot about allies: they would win the war for him and provide the basis for building the peace. The world might indeed come in time to resemble the United States; it was best, hence, to stay involved within it. Not to do so was to leave the way open for "something worse."

In the years since the Cold War ended, there's been a lively debate about what happens when the "something worse" disappears. It was easy enough, while the Soviet Union existed, to see the attractions of living within an American sphere of influence: those had been clear ever since Kennan and the other architects of the Marshall Plan maneuvered Stalin into building the wall that contained him in 1947. The United States went through most of the 1990s, though, without an obvious adversary, and yet with a degree of global hegemony that surpassed even what it had been during the Cold War. There was no serious effort, whether from the European Union, the Chinese, the Russians, or any other state or group of states, to build countervailing centers of power, as balance of power theory might have led one to expect. The reason, very likely, was the habit of self-restraint Americans had developed—because they had had to—during the Cold War, a habit they did not entirely relinquish after it ended.[29]

So when a challenge finally did come, on September 11, 2001, it was not from a state at all, but from a gang. Has Osama bin Laden or his successors or his emulators become the "something worse" that allows the United States, by consent, to sustain and even expand the global hegemony it developed during the Cold War? That certainly seemed to be the case in the immediate aftermath of the attack, when most of the world followed—of all people—the French in proclaiming that "we are all Americans."[30] Since that time, though, that vision of "something worse" has faded, while the actions of the Bush administration have come to be seen, in many parts of the world, as posing a greater threat than anything future terrorists or their allies might do. The reason, I suspect, is the administration's *apparent* reversion to a hegemony based on unilateralism and preemption rather than on multilateralism and self-restraint: a nineteenth-century vision that plays badly at the beginning of the twenty-first. Consent, as a consequence, has proven difficult to sustain.

That poses a problem, because the means we choose in this post-September 11th environment could wind up undermining the ends we seek. It's also possible, though, that the ends we seek, given the new threats we face, can be achieved only by means different from those that won World War II and the Cold War. This much at least is clear: the dilemma is a difficult one, and its resolution will largely determine the relationship between surprise, security, and the American experience in the twenty-first century.

Both the British attack on Washington in 1814 and the Japanese attack on Pearl Harbor in 1941 revealed failures in what we would today call homeland security. The British invasion showed that the United States could no longer rely upon competition among the European great powers to keep it safe: wars in Europe had in the past, and might again, spill over onto the North American continent. The Japanese assault demonstrated that the United States could no longer depend upon continental or even hemispheric hegemony to insulate it from danger: new methods of projecting military strength across great distances meant that the rise of hostile *states* anywhere in the world could endanger our security.

It's important to emphasize that word "states," because it distinguishes the surprises of 1814 and 1941 from the one that occurred in 2001. The first two attacks did indeed come from states using a familiar form of power—military force—in unexpected ways. The remedies fell, therefore, within the traditional limits of diplomacy and warfare. The United States might seek to dissuade, deter, or defeat such adversaries, but whatever option it chose it would be dealing with an identifiable regime led by identifiable leaders operating by identifiable means from an identifiable piece of territory. We could assume, therefore, a more or less common calculation of costs versus benefits across the differences that separated us from our opponents. A sufficient level of diplomatic activity would remove whatever reasons there might be for hostility; if it didn't, a sufficient accumulation of retaliatory capability would deter whoever remained hostile from attacking us; and if that didn't work, a sufficient application of military strength would compel an eventual settlement or surrender.

None of these things was true of the terrorists who carried out the attacks of September 11, 2001. They acted on behalf of no state, for although Al Qaeda was operating from a base in Afghanistan, it's not at all clear that Osama bin Laden consulted his Taliban hosts prior to launching the operation, or that—given the certainty of reprisal—they would have approved it had he done so. Nor can anyone claim that the destruction of the Taliban or the subsequent invasion of Iraq has removed the danger of future terrorist strikes, in the same way that defeating Nazi Germany and imperial Japan in World War II eliminated the threats those regimes posed. Nor is it likely that diplomacy or deterrence could have prevented the September 11th attacks, because those techniques require identifiable adversaries who have interests of their own—whether it be the survival of their regime or simply of themselves—

which they wish to secure. The terrorists struck, as states can never do, from the sanctuary provided by anonymity: how does one negotiate with a shadow? Nor were they interested in their own survival: how does one deter someone who's prepared to commit suicide?

There have always been anarchists, assassins, and saboteurs operating without obvious sponsors, and many of them have been willing to risk their lives in doing so.[1] Single acts of terror, however, have rarely in the past shaken the stability of states or societies because the number of victims they have targeted and the amount of damage they have caused have been relatively small. Even the assassination of the Archduke Franz Ferdinand in Sarajevo in 1914—which is often said to have set off World War I—could not have produced that result had it not also been for the blundering diplomacy, mechanical mobilizations, and widespread public enthusiasm for war that so quickly followed. Terrorists have generally required a long series of attacks, extending over years or even decades, in order to undermine or overthrow a regime. And even then there's no guarantee of success, as the Irish Republican Army, the Palestinian Liberation Organization, the Basque separatists, the Tamil tigers, and the Colombian drug lords have had occasion to discover.

September 11th was something new in this respect also. For

although the attacks did not destabilize a regime—the effect was just the opposite—they certainly did shake a society. No previous act of terrorism had come anywhere close in lives lost and damage inflicted: indeed it would be difficult to think of any conventional military operation in which the results produced were so disproportionate to the resources expended. As President George W. Bush himself pointed out: "All of the chaos and suffering [the terrorists] caused came at much less than the cost of a single tank."[2] Or, to put it another way, by expending 19 lives and a few hundred thousand dollars, the attackers managed to kill some 3,000 people, to inflict as much as a hundred billion dollars' worth of property damage, and to redefine the nature of our times.

Despite our victory in the Cold War, despite a post-Cold War defense budget that far exceeded that of everyone else, despite an economic and cultural predominance that had made the United States, in the words of some of its critics, a "hyper-power," this country had shown itself incapable of protecting its citizens on its own territory as they went about their daily lives.[3] To paraphrase Winston Churchill, never in the history of human endeavor had so many had so much to fear from the actions of so few.

That, at least, is how things looked as Americans sat down at their dinner tables on the evening of September 11, 2001. We seemed to be back to a level of personal insecurity unknown since our ancestors were staking out a society along an advancing frontier, with the protections afforded by government trailing along behind them. The right to live our lives without fearing for our lives—what C. Vann Woodward described as the expectation of "free security"—had been called into question all over again. There was once more, as there had been early in our history, a homeland security deficit, unlike anything we'd experienced in either of the world wars or the Cold War.

The deficit this time extended to other homelands as well, for the attacks could as easily have occurred in any great city on the face of the earth: all were equally undefended. The potential targets, in this new war, were the very fabric—the infrastructure—though which modern societies function. And the possible attackers were almost as ubiquitous, including not just hostile states but also gangs, perhaps even individuals, all of whom were free to choose their own times, places, and methods of striking. September 11th placed what we like to think of as "civilization" itself back on a dangerous frontier, leaving governments everywhere scrambling to catch up.

"The combination of unconventional weapons proliferation with the persistence of international terrorism will end the relative invulnerability of the U.S. homeland to catastrophic attack," the U.S. Commission on National Security/21st Century warned publicly in its final report on March 15, 2001. "A direct attack against American citizens on American soil is likely over the next quarter century."[4] Created by President Bill Clinton in 1997 and co-chaired by former senators Gary Hart and Warren Rudman, the commission was remarkably accurate in anticipating the coming crisis. It was wrong only in that the event it predicted was months—not years—away. When the attack came, nevertheless, the surprise was total.

Part of the explanation lay in the novelty of the methods chosen. No one had ever before used box cutters to hijack airplanes and then crash them into buildings. No one had ever before employed collective suicide on such a scale in the pursuit of mass murder on such a scale. No one had ever before set out with such success to inflict wartime levels of damage in peacetime. Prediction, more often than not, is based on precedents: it's hard to foresee what's never been attempted. It's even harder when what is to be foreseen shatters several precedents at once.

A second reason for the surprise was the classic intelligence problem—also evident at Pearl Harbor—of distinguishing signals from noise.[5] It was easy enough after September 11th to track the movements of the terrorists because their identities were known and their culpability had been established. What distinguished them before the attacks, though, from all the other individuals who might fit a terrorist "profile"? Links to earlier Al Qaeda operations became obvious after New York and Washington were hit; to have seen them beforehand against the cacophony of unrelated events would have been much more difficult. And then there's the fact that terrorists always have the initiative: it's they who determine the time, place, and method of attack. Defenders—even those who knew from the 1993 bombing that the World Trade Center might again be a target—must anticipate all contingencies. Terrorists need provide only one.

The Hart-Rudman report established the nation's vulnerability, but even it could not say when, how, or from where that vulnerability might be tested. Its conclusions, however striking, therefore fell within the realm of the hypothetical. Press coverage was minimal, and the response of the newly installed Bush administration—like that of the outgoing Clinton administration—to the commission's preliminary findings was little more than polite thanks. That the foundations of national security were about suffer a seismic jolt was still by no means clear.

There was yet a third reason for the surprise, though, which went beyond the concerns of Hart-Rudman: it had to do with a widespread sense in the academic and policy communities during the 1990s that the international system had become so benign that the United States no longer faced serious security threats of any kind. Paradoxically, the success of American grand strategy during the Cold War encouraged this view.

The record was indeed impressive. The United States had used military occupations to transform Germany and Japan into thriving capitalist democracies, and the Marshall Plan had secured similar results elsewhere in Europe. Over the next four decades democracy and capitalism spread much more widely, even tentatively into the Soviet Union itself. Meanwhile the world's other great communist state, China, was pulling off a dialectical transformation that neither Marx nor Mao could ever have imagined, becoming a hotbed of capitalism, if not yet of democracy. By the time the Cold War ended, no other models for organizing human society seemed viable: Americans were remaking the world, or so it appeared, to resemble themselves. And the world, it also seemed, was not resisting.

Certain theorists concluded from this that the movement toward democracy and capitalism was irreversible, and that "history" therefore was coming to an end. It might have been an innocuous enough argument, given the care social scientists had taken in recent years to ensure that their theories bore little connection to reality;[6] but this particular theory—associated most closely with the political scientist Francis Fukuyama—did wind up shaping the course of events. The Clinton administration drew from it the idea that if progress toward political self-determination and economic integration was assured, then the United States need only, as national security adviser Anthony Lake put it, "engage" with the rest of the world in order to "enlarge" those processes. The hegemony by consent the United States had won during the Cold War would simply become the post-Cold War international system. President Clinton himself saw little need for a grand strategy under these circumstances. Neither Roosevelt nor Truman had had one, he told a top adviser early in 1994: "they just made it up as they went along."[7]

There were several problems with this position, quite apart from the chief executive's shaky knowledge of World War II and early Cold War strategy. It encouraged a tendency to view history in linear terms, and to ignore the feedback effects that can cause successes to breed failures by inducing complacency—just as failures can breed successes by shattering complacency. It sought coherence through alignment with vague processes rather than through the specification of clear objectives. It brought the Clinton team closer to the examples of Harding and Coolidge than to those of Roosevelt and Truman, for those presidents of the 1920s had also allowed an illusion of safety to produce a *laissez-faire* foreign and national security policy. Finally, Clinton and his advisers assumed the continued primacy of states within the international system. If you could make most of them democratic, if you could bind them together by removing restrictions on trade and investment as well as on the movement of people and ideas, then the causes of violence and the insecurity it breeds would drop away. The argument was well intentioned but shallow.[8]

For what if the power of states themselves was diminishing? What if the very remedies the Clinton model prescribed—political self-determination and economic integration—were slowly undermining the authority of those for whom the prescription had been intended? What if the hidden history of the Cold War was one in which the great powers, under American tutelage, ultimately resolved most of their differences, only to find that their own power was no longer as great as it had once been? It doesn't take a rocket scientist to see how this might have happened.[9]

Self-determination certainly enhances legitimacy: that's why democracies during the Cold War proved more durable than autocracies. But it can also expose an absence of legitimacy, which is what led to the breakup of the Soviet Union, Yugoslavia, and Czechoslovakia after the Cold War. There are now more independent states than ever before—almost 200, as compared to about 50 at the end of World War II—but that doesn't mean that the international state system is stronger. It means just the opposite: that there are more "failed" or "derelict" states than ever before.

Integration certainly enhances prosperity: that's why so many people benefited from the liberalization of trade and investment that took place during and after the Cold War. But the resulting global market has also constrained the ability of states to determine the conditions under which their citizens live. Marx was right in pointing out that although capitalism generates great wealth, it distributes that wealth unevenly. States used to have the capacity to cushion that process, thereby minimizing the resentment it generated: progressivism and the New Deal in the United States, social democracy in Europe, and their equivalents elsewhere provided the social safety nets that saved capitalism from the self-destruction Marx had forecast for it. Now though, in an unregulated global economy, those nets are sagging and becoming frayed.[10]

It's also the case that states—even democracies—used to have some control over movements of people and exchanges of ideas. We tend to celebrate the fact that it's more difficult to impose such restrictions in a world of cheap air travel, liberal immigration policies, fax machines, satellite television transmitters, cell phones, and the internet. But there's also a price, which is that it's harder than it used to be for states to monitor the activities of those individuals, gangs, and networks who are their enemies.

The bottom line, then, is that states are more peaceful these days—that's a major accomplishment of the Cold War—but they're also weaker than they used to be. That situation too contributed to the events of September 11th, and it's certainly shaping the era that has followed. The most important failure of strategic vision in Washington, therefore, lay in the inability of American leaders to look beyond their Cold War victory to the circumstances that might undermine its benefits. As after World War I, they allowed the absence of visible danger to convince them that nothing invisible could pose a threat. They assumed that it was enough simply to have won the game. It did not occur to them that the arena within which the game was being played—together with the rules by which the United States, its allies, and its defeated adversaries had played it—might now be at risk.[11]

It was not just the Twin Towers that collapsed on the morning of September 11, 2001: so too did some of our most fundamental assumptions about international, national, and personal security.

That was the situation President Bush confronted before that morning had ended. Any administration in such a crisis would have had to rethink what it thought it knew about security and hence strategy; but this administration has done so in a particularly startling way, with striking results. To sense how much so, try a time travel exercise: place yourself back on that terrible day and ask how you would have responded had someone predicted the following:

That the United States would quickly respond by invading, and easily conquering, the nation any historian could have told you would be the most resistant to invasion and conquest, Afghanistan—and that it would have the support of the Afghan people and of most of the rest of the world in doing so. That the Bush administration would then, over the next few months, undertake the most fundamental reassessment of American grand strategy in over half a century, and that it would publish the results of this rethinking, for all to read, discuss, and dissent from. That it would then, in a manner fully consistent with that strategy, seek the approval of its allies and the United Nations Security Council for what it regarded as the next logical step—going after Saddam Hussein's Iraq—and that it would fail miserably in getting that approval.

That the United States would then nonetheless, with the help of Great Britain, go ahead and attack Iraq anyway, in the face of the direst warnings about the risks of military resistance, the use of weapons of mass destruction, the eruption of outrage in the Arab world, a new outbreak of terrorism, a huge increase in the price of oil, and astronomical estimates of the human and material costs of the operation—only to have none of these things happen. That among the things that did happen would be: a modest improvement in American and global economic conditions; an intensified dialogue within the Arab world about political reform; a withdrawal of American forces from Saudi Arabia along with their redeployment to such formerly inhospitable locations as Afghanistan, Iraq, Uzbekistan, Kyrgzstan, Romania, and Bulgaria; and an increasing nervousness on the part of the Syrian and Iranian governments as they contemplated the consequences of being surrounded by American clients or surrogates.[12]

Finally, that much of the rest of the world would find itself amazed, and if truth be told somewhat alarmed, over the emergence of the United States as a *more* powerful and purposeful actor within the international system than it had been on September 11, 2001—as well as over one of the most surprising transformations of an underrated national leader since Prince Hal became Henry V.[13] If anyone had predicted all of this on that day, you might have wondered what pills they'd been popping or what weed they'd been smoking. You almost certainly would not have taken them seriously. And yet, this is indeed what's happened.

So how much of it reflects planning, and how much the role of luck, improvisation, or accident? Determining that balance is always tricky, but in this instance the Bush administration's strategic reassessment provides clear evidence that planning has taken place. And despite their reputation for secrecy, the Bush planners have been—for the most part—candid about what they've been doing. It would be a mistake, therefore, not to pay careful attention to what they've said. A good place to start is the president's report on *The National Security Strategy of the United States of America* (NSS), released on September 17, 2002; that statement in turn elaborated on an important but little-reported speech Bush gave at West Point on June 1, 2002.[14]

Beginnings, in such documents, tell you a lot. The Bush NSS sets three tasks for post-September 11th American grand strategy: "We will defend the peace by fighting terrorists and tyrants. We will preserve the peace by building good relations among the great powers. We will extend the peace by encouraging free and open societies on every continent."[15] It's worth comparing these priorities with the three the Clinton administration put forth in its final report on national security strategy, published in December, 1999: "To enhance America's security. To bolster America's economic prosperity. To promote democracy and human rights abroad."[16]

The differences are instructive. The Bush objectives specify defending, preserving, and extending peace; the Clinton statement seems simply to assume peace. Bush calls for cooperation among the great powers; Clinton never uses that term. Bush specifies the encouragement of free and open societies on every continent; Clinton contents himself with "promoting" democracy and human rights "abroad." Even in these first lines, then, the Bush NSS comes across as more forceful, more carefully crafted, and—unexpectedly—more multilateral than its immediate predecessor. It's a tip-off that there're interesting things going on here.

Defense against tyrants, of course, is nothing new: that's what our World War II and Cold War strategy was all about. What is new is Bush's elevation of the terrorist threat to the level of that posed by tyrants. This recalculation of danger reflects the fact that the United States no longer confronts adversaries armed with thousands of nuclear weapons and the means of delivering them almost instantaneously. But it also responds to a previously underestimated threat from terrorists, for if box cutters and civilian airliners can become weapons of mass destruction, what other grim possibilities might there be? The extent of potential damage is, by Cold War standards, vastly diminished: we aren't likely to see mushroom clouds rising throughout the northern hemisphere. The likelihood of damage—on a scale comparable to or even worse than what happened on September 11th—is, however, significantly increased.[17]

The reason for this, the Bush NSS points out, is that terrorists tend not to behave in the way that states do. Because hostile states have interests at stake and territories to defend, credible threats of retaliation will normally deter and contain them: if the Cold War demonstrated anything at all, it was surely this. Terrorists, for whom terror is an end in itself and death is no deterrent, behave very differently; nor are they easily identifiable. Dangerous states, whatever the dangers they pose, can't hide. Terrorists can and do.[18]

When you add to these new threats two legacies left over from the Cold War—the declining authority of the international state system, and the proliferation of weapons of mass destruction—the world begins to look far less hospitable than it had seemed to be only a few years earlier when there was talk of history coming to an end. "We cannot defend America and our friends by hoping for the best," Bush warns, in a scarcely veiled criticism of his predecessor. "History will judge harshly those who saw this coming danger but failed to act."[19]

What all of this implies, then, is a redefinition, for only the third time in American history, of what it will take to protect the nation from surprise attack. That requirement has expanded now from John Quincy Adams's vision of continental hegemony through Franklin D. Roosevelt's conception of a great power coalition aimed at containing, deterring, and if necessary defeating aggressor states to what is already being called the Bush Doctrine: that the United States will identify and eliminate terrorists wherever they are, together with the regimes that sustain them.[20] Respecting sovereignty is no longer sufficient because that implies a game in which the players understand and respect the rules. In this new game there are no rules.

The Bush Doctrine does not reject deterrence and containment. It does, however, insist upon the need to supplement these familiar strategies with one that sounds, to modern ears, unfamiliar: that of preemption. In fact, preemption sounds new only because it's old: it's a nineteenth-century concept, rooted in concerns about security along the nation's expanding borders. The "terrorists" of that day caused Americans on the frontier to fear for their lives. Today's terrorists provoke similar anxieties, but the frontiers now can be anywhere, which means that targets can be everywhere. September 11th showed that deterrence and containment alone won't work against such adversaries: that's why preemption is necessary. As the Bush NSS puts it, in language Adams might well have applauded: "We cannot let our enemies strike first."[21]

The NSS is careful to specify a legal basis for preemption: international law recognizes "that nations need not suffer an attack before they can lawfully take action to defend themselves against forces that present an imminent danger of attack." There's also a preference for preempting multilaterally: "The United States will constantly strive to enlist the support of the international community." But "we will not hesitate to act alone, if necessary, to exercise our right of self-defense by acting preemptively against such terrorists, to prevent them from doing harm against our people and our country."[22]

Preemption, in turn, requires something else of which Adams would have approved, which is hegemony: the capacity to act wherever one needs to without significant resistance from rival states. Although Bush speaks, in his letter of introduction to the NSS, of creating "a balance of power that favors freedom" while forsaking "unilateral advantage," the body of that document makes it clear that such a balance as traditionally conceived is not what he has in mind. He promises sufficient strength "to dissuade potential adversaries from pursuing a military build-up in hopes of surpassing, or equaling, the power of the United States."[23] The West Point speech put it more bluntly: "America has, and intends to keep, strengths beyond challenge."[24]

How, though, will the rest of the world respond to American hegemony? That gets us to another innovation in the Bush strategy, which is its emphasis on cooperation among great powers.

There's a contrast here with Clinton's focus on justice for small powers, as reflected in the decisions to expand NATO and to go to war in Kosovo, both made against the wishes of the Russians. The argument also seems at odds, at first glance, with maintaining military strength beyond challenge, for don't the weak always unite to oppose the strong? In theory, yes, but in practice and in history, not necessarily. Here the Bush team seems to have absorbed some pretty sophisticated political science, for one of the issues that discipline has been wrestling with recently is why there's still no anti-American coalition despite the overwhelming dominance of the United States in the years since the Cold War ended.[25]

Bush suggests two explanations, both of which most political scientists—not all—would find plausible. The first is that the other great powers actually *prefer* management of the international system by a single hegemon as long as it's a relatively benign one. When there's only one super-power, there's no point for anyone else to try to compete with it in military capabilities. International conflict shifts to trade rivalries and other relatively minor quarrels, none of them worth fighting about.[26] Compared with what great powers have done to one another in the past, this is no bad thing.

American hegemony is also acceptable because it's linked to certain values that all states and cultures—if not all terrorists and tyrants—share. "Targeting innocent civilians for murder is always and everywhere wrong," Bush insisted at West Point. "Brutality against women is always and everywhere wrong." And as the NSS added: "No people on earth yearn to be oppressed, aspire to servitude, or eagerly await the midnight knock of the secret police."[27] It's this association of unchallengeable strength with universal principles, Bush argues, that will cause the other great powers to go along with whatever the United States has to do to preempt the actions of terrorists and tyrants, even if it does so alone. For, as was the case throughout the Cold War, there's something worse out there than American hegemony.

The final innovation in the Bush strategy deals with the longer-term issue of removing the causes of terrorism and tyranny altogether. Here again the administration's thinking parallels an emerging consensus within the scholarly community, which is that it wasn't poverty that caused a group of middle-class and reasonably well-educated Middle Easterners to fly three airplanes into buildings and another into the ground. It was, rather, frustrations growing out of the absence of representative institutions within their own societies, so that the only outlet for dissent was religious fanaticism.[28]

Bush's solution to this complex problem is breathtakingly simple: it is to spread democracy everywhere. His administration differs from its predecessor in two important ways: it regards the objective as achievable within the foreseeable future, but it does not see the process as automatic—as something we can simply sit back and wait for. The risks from terrorism no longer allow that luxury. So the formula is to be Fukuyama plus force: the United States must now finish the job that Woodrow Wilson started. The world, quite literally, is to be made safe for democracy, even those parts of it, like the Muslim Middle East, that have so far resisted that tendency. Terrorism—and by implication the authoritarianism that breeds it—must become as obsolete as slavery, piracy, or genocide: "behavior that no respectable government can condone or support and that all must oppose."[29] Otherwise democracy, in this new age of vulnerability, will never be safe in the world.

This is, then, a radically different grand strategy from what we've seen in recent years. It rejects the Clinton administration's assumption that because the movement toward democracy and capitalism had become irreversible, all the United States had to do was to "engage" with the rest of the world to "enlarge" that process. Its parts for the most part interconnect: there's a coherence in the Bush strategy that the Clinton national security team—notable for its simultaneous cultivation and humiliation of Russia[30]— never achieved. It sees no contradiction between the wielding of power and commitment to principles: unusually for conservatives but in the tradition of Ronald Reagan, it is optimistic about human nature, and therefore Wilsonian in its view of the world.[31] Finally, its architects tend to speak plainly, at times bluntly, with little concern for euphemism or "nuance." Like John Quincy Adams, they see no point in employing hypocrisy to cloak ambition.

There are, however, certain aspects of the Bush strategy about which the administration does not speak openly. These have to do with why it regards tyrants, in the post-September 11th world, as at least as dangerous as terrorists—despite the fact that it has failed, as yet, to connect any tyrant with the events of that day.

Bush first tried to answer this question in his January 2002 State of the Union address when he warned that an "axis of evil" made up of Iraq, Iran, and North Korea was accumulating weapons of mass destruction which could be used to commit terrorist acts.[32] The phrase was colorful but not clear, because Saddam Hussein, the Iranian mullahs, and Kim Jong Il were hardly the only tyrants around who had dabbled with dangerous weaponry, nor were their ties to one another or to Al Qaeda apparent. Nor did Bush explain why containment and deterrence would not work against these tyrants, since they were all more into survival than suicide. Their lifestyles tended more toward palaces than caves.[33]

After several months of repeating the rhetoric without resolving these issues, the administration fell silent on the "axis of evil." Neither the West Point speech nor the NSS repeated the phrase, leaving the suspicion that it originated in overzealous speech-writing rather than careful thought: in an ill-advised effort, per-haps, to make the president sound simultaneously like FDR and Reagan. By the beginning of 2003, the administration was stress-ing the *differences* in its policies toward the Iraqis, the Iranians, and the North Koreans, rather than their similarities to one an-other. All of which left open the question of why, having buried the "axis of evil," Bush remained so keen on burying Saddam Hussein.

It patronizes the administration to explain its Iraqi preoccupa-tion in terms of filial obligation. Despite his comment that Saddam was the "guy who tried to kill my dad," George W. Bush was no Hamlet, agonizing over how to meet a tormented parental ghost's demands for revenge.[34] Shakespeare might still help, though, if you shift the analogy to Henry V. For that monarch understood the psychological value of victory—of defeating an adversary suf-ficiently thoroughly that you shatter the confidence of others, so that they'll roll over themselves before you have to roll over them.

For Henry, the demonstration was Agincourt, the famous vic-tory over the French in 1415. The Bush administration got a taste of Agincourt with its victory over the Taliban at the end of 2001, to which the Afghans responded by gleefully shaving their beards, shedding their burkas, and cheering the infidels—even to the point of lending them horses from which they laser-marked bomb targets. Suddenly, it seemed, American values were transportable to the remotest and most alien parts of the earth. The vision that opened up was not the one of clashing civilizations we'd been led to expect from the writings of Samuel P. Huntington, Fukuyama's chief rival in predicting the shape of the post-Cold War world. Rather, as the NSS put it, what was happening was a clash "inside a civilization, a battle for the future of the Muslim world."[35]

How, though, to maintain the momentum, given that the Taliban was no more and that Al Qaeda wasn't likely to present itself as a conspicuous target? This was where Saddam Hussein came in: Iraq was the most feasible place in which to strike the next blow. If we could topple that tyrant, if we could repeat the Afghan Agincourt along the banks of the Tigris and the Euphrates, then we could accomplish a great deal. We could complete the task the Gulf War left unfinished. We could destroy whatever weapons of mass destruction Saddam might have accumulated since. We could end whatever support he was providing for terrorists beyond Iraq's borders, notably those who acted against Israel. We could liberate the Iraqi people. We could ensure an ample supply of inexpensive oil. We could set in motion a process that could undermine and ultimately remove reactionary regimes elsewhere in the

Middle East, thereby eliminating the principal breeding ground for terrorism. And, as President Bush did say publicly in a powerful speech to the United Nations on September 12, 2002, we could save that organization from the irrelevance into which it would otherwise descend if its resolutions continued to be contemptuously disregarded.[36] The attraction of this particular stone was the number of birds it could simultaneously kill.

This was then, in every sense, a *grand* strategy. What appeared at first to be a lack of clarity about who was deterrable and who wasn't turned out to be a plan for transforming the entire Muslim Middle East: for bringing it, once and for all, into the modern world. There'd been nothing like this in boldness, sweep, and vision since Americans took it upon themselves, more than half a century ago, to democratize Germany and Japan, thus setting in motion processes that stopped short of only a few places on earth, one of which was the Muslim Middle East.

The *grandness* of a strategy, however, by no means ensures its success. We've had examples in the past of ambitiously conceived and carefully crafted strategies failing, most conspicuously the Nixon-Kissinger attempt, during the early 1970s, to bring the Soviet Union into an international system of satisfied states. There have been instances of carelessly improvised strategies succeeding: the Clinton administration accomplished that feat in Kosovo in 1999. The greatest theorist of strategy, Carl von Clausewitz, repeatedly emphasized in his writings the role of chance, which can at times defeat the best of designs and at other times hand victory to the worst of them. There is as well the problem of perspective: what may appear as triumphs to contemporaries can look very different to those who follow.[37]

Any assessment of the Bush grand strategy at this point, therefore, must be tentative in the extreme. It's too early to know how historians will evaluate this new American approach to the world—or even, more immediately, how adversaries, allies, and the American people will do so. It is possible now, though, to compare promises with performance so far: to what extent have the first attempts to implement the Bush strategy borne out the expectations of its designers?

Their most obvious failure has to do with the relationship between *preemption, hegemony, and consent.* The Bush NSS acknowledged the multiplier effects of multilateralism,[38] and the administration worked hard to secure these in the months preceding the war in Iraq. For a time it appeared to be succeeding. Responding to Bush's challenge, the United Nations Security Council passed a resolution in November 2002 requiring Iraq to honor the commitment it had made after the 1991 Gulf War to dismantle its weapons of mass destruction, and to readmit the international inspectors it had thrown out in 1998. Rejection by Saddam Hussein would have constituted the "smoking gun"—or, to put it in FDR's terms, "the first shot"—that would have permitted the United States, at the head of a United Nations coalition, to invade the country.

The Iraqi dictator, however, failed to follow that script. He grudgingly allowed the inspectors back in and went through the motions, at least, of complying with the Security Council resolution. His actions raised enough hope for a peaceful settlement among the other members of that organization to undermine the unity the Americans and their British allies had achieved there—this despite the fact that it had been their own military buildup in the Kuwaiti desert that had induced Iraqi cooperation in the first place.

Meanwhile, that buildup was creating its own problems, for having deployed their forces, the Americans and the British could not leave them deployed indefinitely. Military operations would have to begin before the hot weather did. The demands of this logistical and meteorological timetable caused others to be compressed, with damaging results for the Bush administration's efforts to maintain multilateral support. One such schedule was that of the United Nations inspectors, who asked for more time to complete their work. Washington's reluctance to grant it shook the already fragile consensus within the Security Council, which in turn led Bush, Prime Minister Tony Blair, and their advisers to cut another set of corners involving their own intelligence estimates on Iraqi weapons of mass destruction. The alarming assessments they cited publicly seemed strained at the time and have proven since to have been wrong: there were no such weapons in anything like a usable state.[39] As a result, these claims failed to rebuild support within the Security Council. They also diminished, in advance, the credibility of whatever future intelligence claims Bush and Blair might make.

So in the end, consensus collapsed: in striking contrast to what had happened when the first Bush administration led the military campaign to eject Saddam's forces from Kuwait twelve years earlier, no other great power joined the United States and Great Britain when they invaded Iraq on March, 20, 2003. Nor was there—owing to the threat of French and Russian vetoes—a Security Council resolution authorizing the operation, as there had been in 1991. Regional allies like Saudi Arabia, Egypt, and Pakistan backed away from open military cooperation, and even Turkey—a hitherto reliable member of NATO—at the last moment denied the use of its territory in staging the attack. The invasion would up being carried out by American and British forces operating out of Kuwait, alongside much smaller units from Australia, Poland, and South Korea. Bush and Blair were reduced to welcoming the rhetorical support of such states as Micronesia, thereby making their "coalition of the willing" more of a joke than a reality.[40]

From a military perspective, the war in Iraq nonetheless went at least as well as the one in Afghanistan. It too produced its Agincourt moments, most memorably on April 9th, when American marines helped enthusiastic Iraqis topple the giant statue of Saddam Hussein in central Baghdad. Euphoria over this military success could not conceal the fact, however, that a major diplomatic failure had occurred—one that challenged a fundamental premise of the Bush grand strategy. For the decision to go to war in the face of overwhelming opposition abroad—though not, if the polls could be believed, at home—could not help but raise doubts about the rest of the world's willingness to accept American hegemony when used to accomplish preemption. And yet the strategy had called for just such consent: preemption without it might still occur, but only as a last resort.[41]

So why did the Bush administration push so hard for an invasion of Iraq in the spring of 2003 when the dangers Saddam Hussein's regime posed were neither clear nor present, and when the risks of haste were so great? To understand this, I think we need to consider another aspect of the Bush grand strategy, which was its reliance on momentum, or *shock and awe*.

The term became famous in the military press briefings that preceded the war,[42] but I use it here to characterize the determination of the Bush strategists to shake up a status quo in the Middle East that had become dangerous to the security of the United States. The invasions of Afghanistan and Iraq were meant to topple selected dominos with a view to destabilizing others. The purpose was as much psychological as military: to eliminate individuals, gangs, and regimes who commit or support terrorism, but also to intimidate those who might be thinking about doing so. If future terrorist acts were to carry with them the certainty of devastating reprisal, then that should generate resistance to those acts within the societies that spawned them—possibly even before they had been committed.[43] Preemption, by this logic, could produce a deterrent effect that could allow a return to containment. In order for this new domino theory to work, however, the pace had to be kept up: there couldn't be too much time between topplings.

The problem with this strategy was that it rattled more dominos than intended. Open talk of preemption in the NSS and elsewhere was unsettling allies abroad and critics at home well before the Iraqi war broke out, for although the United States had never abandoned the right to preempt in the face of danger, it had not publicly asserted that right for almost a century. It was one thing for a continental hegemon to threaten preemption within its own environs, as John Quincy Adams, Theodore Roosevelt, and Woodrow Wilson had all done.[44] It was quite another thing for a global hegemon to threaten it wherever necessary, as George W. Bush appeared to be doing. It's hardly surprising, therefore, that the resulting shock and awe extended beyond its Middle Eastern targets.

What had sustained broad if not universal consent to the wielding of American power during World War II and the Cold War was the prospect of something worse—the possible victory of an authoritarian alternative. What sustained it after that danger had passed in the 1990s may well have been the Clinton administration's non-threatening non-strategy of "engagement" and "enlargement." What sustained it in the immediate aftermath of September 11th was a near-universal sense of horror and sympathy, together with a widespread consensus that retaliation against Al Qaeda and the Taliban was deserved, proportionate, and therefore just.

The rush to war in Iraq in the absence of a "first shot" or a "smoking gun" left a very different impression: a growing sense throughout much of the world that there could be *nothing worse* than American hegemony if it was to be used in this way. For if Washington could go against the wishes of the United Nations and most of its own allies in invading Iraq, what could it *not* do? What were to be, henceforth, the constraints on its power? It does no good to dismiss such sentiments on the grounds that those who hold them are acting emotionally, for their own cynical reasons, or because they are French: the motives that lie behind attitudes make them no less real, nor do they mitigate consequences. Among these was the fact that, within a little more than a year and a half, the United States exchanged its long-established reputation as the principal *stabilizer* of the international system for one as its chief *destabilizer.* This was heavy price to pay to sustain momentum, however great the need for it may have been.

Shock and awe are necessarily departures from the normal. If successful, they can even shift what "normal" is. But they can't sustain the gains they produce because the effect wears off. They become what's expected, and that undermines the element of surprise that makes such practices work in the first place.

That's why good strategists know when to stop shocking and awing: when to begin consolidating the benefits these strategies have provided. The classic example is Otto von Bismarck, who set new standards for shock and awe by provoking three wars—against

Denmark in 1864, Austria in 1866, and France in 1870—all with a view to clearing the way for the unification of Germany. Having accomplished this in 1871, he replaced his destabilizing strategy with a new one aimed at consolidation and reassurance—at persuading his defeated enemies as well as nervous allies and alarmed bystanders that they would be better off living within the new system he had imposed on them than by continuing to fight or fear it. The revolutionary had become a conservative.[45]

Bad strategists don't know when to make this switch. They become so enamored of shock and awe that it becomes an end in itself for them. Because they're incapable of providing reassurance, they wind up being system destroyers rather than system builders. Napoleon and Hitler fell into this trap, as did the man who finally fired Bismarck, Kaiser Wilhelm II. Reassurance is critical because in its absence fear sooner or later gives way to friction which gives way to resistance. That's why Clausewitz, in *On War,* gave equal attention to the power to act and the capacity to impede. It's also why that most formidable of modern strategists, Sir Winston Churchill, began each volume of his great history of World War II with the admonition: "In victory, magnanimity."

It's too soon to say into which of these categories the United States victory in Iraq will fall, but the early indicators have not been encouraging. The raggedness with which its military forces ran the initial occupation contrasted strikingly with their efficiency in invading that country: consolidation obviously had not been a planning priority. Rhetoric too was ragged: there was no clear voice for reassurance—whether to enemies, allies, or bystanders—within an administration that has never deployed language with anything like the care it has taken in deploying its military capabilities.[46] Churchill, a master of the relationship between language and strategy, would not have approved. Intimidation in strategy has its place but also its risks: it's like running your tachometer into its red zone. There may be times when you need to do it, but if you make it a habit you shouldn't expect your vehicle to get you to where you want to go.

An even more serious gap between promise and performance could emerge from an as yet untested premise within the Bush grand strategy: having undertaken to remake the Middle East, does it have the blueprint right? *Is democracy indeed the path to security in that part of the world?*[47] The administration has answered this question affirmatively with enough frequency and force that I don't doubt its sincerity. What if it's wrong, though? What if terrorism—and the region's more general anti-Americanism—do not originate in a democratic deficit, but in more complex and therefore less definable causes?

This of course has been Huntington's argument for over a decade: that democratization and globalization have by no means eroded "civilizational" differences; that nowhere do these run deeper than in the Middle East; and that the security of the United States and other democratic societies depends upon *not* trying to impose their own values on cultures where they cannot possibly take root, but rather on maintaining the "multicivilizational character of global politics."[48] The Bush NSS had two responses to Huntington, both of them persuasive. One was its argument that in a post-September 11th world the old Cold War model of coexisting with adversaries would not work: these new adversaries had demonstrated all too painfully that they were not prepared to coexist with us. The other response was the reminder of clashes taking place *within* the Islamic world: if Muslims themselves were divided on the virtues of modernization, then who was to say that democratization could not eventually work for them?[49]

The NSS did not, however, have a clear answer for Fareed Zakaria, who has questioned the connection the administration assumes between order, prosperity, and justice on the one hand—what he calls "liberalism"—and democracy on the other. Tyrannies of the majority, he points out, have a very long history.[50] There are far too many examples of majorities who have embraced disastrous economic policies, abused the rights of minorities, and otherwise sanctioned violence and terrorism for democracy alone to be the remedy for the problems of the Middle East—or anywhere else. The alternative is what Zakaria calls "liberal autocracy": systems like those in China, Taiwan, Singapore, Indonesia, Thailand, Chile, and—interestingly—the European Union, that have shown themselves capable of the long-term planning necessary for political stabilization and economic modernization while avoiding the distractions and volatilities of democratic politics. Even American and British democracy did not emerge overnight: there were decades, in the latter case centuries, of undemocratic preparation.[51]

Zakaria's argument is controversial, especially its insistence that liberal autocracies outperform democracies economically.[52] But it is a useful corrective to the Bush administration's sweeping assumptions about democratic transferability: assumptions, one cannot help but suspect, that account at least in part for its failure to think more deeply about the problems of occupation and administration it would encounter in Iraq—as well as Afghanistan. It also poses a tough question the administration has not yet answered: would the United States be prepared today to risk free elections in those two countries—or anywhere else apart from Israel in the Middle East—in the expectation that they would return governments prepared to cooperate with the United States in restraining terrorists and removing the conditions that breed them? If the answer is "no," or even "not yet," then Zakaria's argument deserves greater attention in Washington than it has so far received.

There is, of course, one time-tested solution for the problem Zakaria has identified, which is *empire*. I mean by this a situation in which a single state shapes the behavior of others, whether directly or indirectly, partially or completely, by means that can range from the outright use of force through intimidation, dependency, inducements, and even inspiration.[53] How else have great powers imposed their authority in the past when confronted with anarchy, resistance, ethnic rivalries, cultural differences, and disparities in economic development? Empires have a bad reputation in this post-colonial age because of the oppression they inflicted. It's worth remembering, though, that they also at times brought order, prosperity, and justice—Zakaria's prerequisites for liberty, and therefore democracy.[54] Where the modern Middle East fits within this range of results is debatable; but the fact that a debate about the merits of empire is even taking place now suggests that imperial solutions (carrying some more politically correct name, to be sure) may be at least as likely as the democratic ones the Bush administration says it's seeking.[55] If that's the case—if we wind up constructing a new American empire in that part of the world—then

that would appear at first glance to be the biggest gap of all between promises made and performance delivered.

▲ ▼

Until you place the Bush grand strategy within the larger context of
American history, where the idea of an "empire of liberty" has
deep roots. The term was Jefferson's, but the conviction that lay
behind it—that empire and liberty are indeed *compatible*—was
widely held in the early republic.[56] Its origins lay, first, in the belief
that the American system of government, unlike any other in the
world at that time, assumed the universality of human rights, so
that people living outside of it would want to be included within it
or, failing that, to emulate it. An empire expanding because of its
own attractiveness would, therefore, safeguard liberty. There was
also the expectation that trade—an activity at which Americans
excelled—would overcome the barriers mercantilism had erected
against it, so that an empire based on mutual economic advantage
could develop: it too would be compatible with liberty. Finally,
there was a defensive motive for this linkage: it arose out of the
conviction that the security of American institutions *required* their
expansion. The liberty the republican experiment had produced
could only flourish within an empire that provided safety.

The first great surprise attack in American history—the British burning of Washington in 1814—powerfully reinforced this last idea: there emerged, as a result, the John Quincy Adams strategy of seeking control over the North American continent, by unilateral means where possible, through preemptive action where necessary. The architects of this continental empire sought to make it an instrument of liberty by granting statehood to their newly acquired territories, thereby bringing them within the constitutional and legal framework under which all Americans lived. Where this was not feasible, as in the cases of Canada and what was left of Mexico after 1848, they halted the expansion. Apart from two glaring exceptions—the persistence of slavery, and the persecution of native Americans—there was no compelling desire to construct a formal empire against the wishes of those to be included within it. The acquisition of the Philippines half a century later did, to be sure, violate this principle; but that event proved to be an anomaly, not a pattern for the future. Military interventions in Mexico, Central America, and the Caribbean during the early twentieth century produced no colonies but rather a sphere of influence in which local sovereignty survived—even if not always respected. The preferred form of empire for the United States through the end of the 1930s remained one based on continental hegemony, ideological example, and commercial opportunity. It did not rely, to the extent that most other empires have, upon continuous coercion, with the abridgement of liberty that practice brings.

The second great surprise attack, at Pearl Harbor in 1941, forced a reconsideration of American grand strategy, but not of the conviction that empire and liberty could coexist. The military and economic strength of the United States would be employed now, not just to dominate North America or even the western hemisphere, but to restore an international balance of power in which democracies would be secure. The defeat of Nazi Germany and imperial Japan in World War II partially accomplished this objective; the successful containment of the Soviet Union and its Marxist-Leninist allies completed the process. The United States acquired, as a result, an expanded sphere of influence that amounted to *informal* empire on a global scale. Because its purpose was to resist authoritarianism, however, Americans saw few conflicts with liberty. Most non-Americans living within that empire during the Cold War saw things similarly, for there was always much worse to fear.[57]

The third and most recent surprise attack—that of September 11, 2001—made it clear that surviving authoritarian regimes, even if feeble or failing, can breed terrorists capable of attacking the United States with devastating results on its own soil. The Bush administration, therefore, has called for yet another expansion of the empire of liberty: it can no longer respect the sovereignty of *any* state that harbors terrorists; it must preempt such threats wherever they appear; it will extend democracy everywhere. The precedent John Quincy Adams set has at last produced what he warned against: an American government that deliberately goes abroad in search of monsters to destroy—lest those monsters attempt to destroy it. It's here, then, that the Adams legacy and the Bush strategy part company, for such a quest, Adams feared, would make the United States the "dictatress of the world." Bush, in contrast, sees the United States as securing liberty throughout the world.

Whatever one thinks of that argument, the expansion of American power in response to surprise attack has no historical precedents: a nation that began with the belief that it could not be safe as long as pirates, marauders, and the agents of predatory empires remained active along its borders has now taken the position that it cannot be safe as long as terrorists and tyrants remain active anywhere in the world. That conclusion surely reflects prudence: where the nation's security is at stake, one can hardly be too careful. It also reflects capability: what other nation today could conceivably aspire to such a role? But it reflects arrogance as well: there's more than a whiff of grandiosity about the insistence that one nation's security is coterminous with that of everyone else. What space is left for the American empire to expand into the next time there's a surprise attack? The self-servingness reflected in these reflections suggests the need for Americans themselves to reflect, long, hard, and carefully—as Adams would have wished them to—about where their empire of liberty is headed.

A good place to start might be with Adam Smith, who saw as early as 1776 that the Americans "are employed in contriving a new form of government for an extensive empire, which, they flatter themselves, will become, and which, indeed, seems very likely to become, one of the greatest and most formidable that ever was in the world."[58] *The Wealth of Nations,* in which that passage appeared, made the case that a collective good—prosperity—required the pursuit of individual interests within an open market. For the state or anyone else to try to determine those interests, or to restrict the choices allowed in pursuing them, or to incorporate them within some central plan—to attempt any of those things, Smith argued, would constitute an abridgment of liberty, the single individual interest everyone shares. In an increasingly complex world, he insisted, no authority possessed the competence to determine and then fulfill each individual's interest. People could, however, be trusted to do their own determining and fulfilling, as long as they proceeded within a set of rules designed to safeguard their right to do so and the fairness with which they went about it.

Although we don't often think of it in this way, the United

States Constitution transferred Smith's thinking from the realm of economics into that of politics. For it too assumed that the pursuit of individual interests within a fixed set of rules would produce a collective good: that's what federalism was all about. It was at the same time, however, no prescription for paralysis. It would be absurd, Alexander Hamilton noted in the 23rd *Federalist,* to confide "to a government the direction of the most essential national interests, without daring to trust it to the authorities which are indispensable to their proper and efficient management. . . . [This] is the strongest argument in favor of an energetic government; for any other can certainly never preserve the Union of so large an empire."[59]

A century and a half later, the United States projected its federal model abroad as it assumed international responsibilities, at first unsuccessfully in the form of Wilson's League of Nations, then more successfully through the United Nations, and most successfully of all through the consensual coalition American leaders built and maintained throughout the Cold War for the purpose of containing international communism. At no point was there an effort to centralize all decision-making in a single location, or to entrust it to a single individual. At no point did power alone confer legitimacy: just as the Constitution gave Delaware an equal voice with Pennsylvania in the United States Senate, so Luxembourg was accorded the same status as France, West Germany, and Great Britain within the North Atlantic Treaty Organization. At no point as well, though, was paralysis permitted: in a manner fully consistent with the spirit of federalism, the American system of Cold War alliances balanced the leadership needed in seeking a common good against the flexibility required to satisfy individual interests.[60] It provided a way for the United States to wield power while minimizing arrogance, and that's not a bad model for an even more powerful United States in a post-September 11th world.[61]

If this record confirms, as I think it does, the "transferability" of Smith's principles into geopolitics as well as politics, then it would seem to follow that a twenty-first-century empire of liberty should not content itself with making the world safe for democracy, or for diversity, or even primarily for the United States. Rather, it should seek to make the world safe for *federalism*, from which all the rest would flow. Adam Smith's grand design—applied more widely than even his prophetic sensibility could ever have imagined—has served this country in particular, as well as the cause of freedom in general, remarkably well. All the more reason, then, not to discard it lightly now that Americans have the opportunity once again to do so much designing.

# AN EVENING AT YALE

No design is likely to succeed, though, in the absence of standards. I can think of no better one for American grand strategy for the twenty-first century than to continue to merit Abraham Lincoln's characterization of the United States, in the middle of the nineteenth century, as "the last best hope of earth."[1] It's startling—but surely accurate—to realize that if all boundary restrictions were removed and everyone who wanted to move could do so freely, the United States would remain the country to which most of the people in most of the rest of the world would choose to come.[2] For however imperial we've become, we have held on to liberty. Lincoln, as in so many other things, had it right. We are, if not the last hope of earth, then certainly in the eyes of most of its inhabitants still the best.

What does that mean, though, for those of us who've been fortunate enough already to have crossed the borders that brought us to this place? What are the responsibilities that come with such a position? What are the dangers?

We saw the latter on September 11, 2001. The question "Why do they hate us so?" was a reasonable one to ask at the time, but as we've learned more about the attackers it's become clear that the better question would have been: "Why do so few hate us so much that they would strike at us in that way?" It wasn't poverty, injustice, or any other morally justifiable grievance that caused them to do so. It was because they agreed with Lincoln. We are, therefore, like the Twin Towers, an irresistible target for those few whose aspiration is to kill hope.

How, then, do we keep hope alive when the costs and risks of doing so have suddenly become much greater? The first thing I'd say is that we have to be ready to fight for it. I shall always remember one of my Yale undergraduates getting up before a group of students and faculty one evening shortly after September 11th and announcing: "I love this country. I love this place. I love what we're doing here tonight. I love it so much that I'm prepared to defend our right to do it, which is why I'm joining the Marines. It's people like me who make it possible for people like you to be here doing what you're doing."

And so, indeed, it is. Our ability as a democracy to question *all* values depends upon our faith in and our determination to defend *certain* values. They are the bedrock beliefs that make it possible for us to be here and for so many others to wish to be. Of course these are social constructions, as my post-modernist colleagues would be quick to point out, *but it's our society that constructed them*. That makes them worth fighting for, as so many others have done before us.

We keep hope alive, as well, by taking responsibility. There's not the slightest doubt in my mind that the world was a better place at the end of the twentieth century because the United States rejected its earlier isolationism and assumed global responsibilities during it. Who else was there to hold the line against the authoritarians who otherwise would have dominated that century? Who else is there now, at the beginning of the twenty-first?

The essence of responsibility, however, is remembering what the ancients taught us about the sin of pride. Which is to say that we badly need mirrors. Which is to say that we need always to see ourselves as others see us. Which is to say that you can't sustain hegemony without consent. Which is to say that consent requires the existence of an alternative more frightening than your own hegemony. Which is to say that that was how American global leadership came about in the twentieth century: it was partly skill and partly luck, but always the fact that there was something worse.

That's still the case at the beginning of the twenty-first century, and it's important to keep it that way. The key to American influence in the world has always been the hope for a better life that we still, more credibly than anyone else, have to offer. The Founding Fathers had hope in mind when they crafted the most durable ideology in modern history. Lincoln evoked that hope at what seemed a hopeless time for this nation. Woodrow Wilson and Franklin D. Roosevelt held out hope in what seemed to be a hopelessly war-torn world. We need to hang onto hope as we prepare for the new era of insecurity we've entered and as we remember the tragedy that brought it about.

All of which brings me around at last to answering a question another of my undergraduates asked in the dark and fearful days that followed September 11th: "Would it be OK now for us to be patriotic?"

Yes, I think it would.

NOTES AND INDEX

## 2 . T H E  N I N E T E E N T H  C E N T U R Y

1. C. Vann Woodward, "The Age of Reinterpretation," *American Historical Review,* 66 (October 1960), 2, 6.

2. Lawrence Freedman, *The Evolution of Nuclear Strategy* (New York: St. Martin's Press, 1983), pp. 225–56, provides a good explanation of how the mutual assured destruction doctrine emerged.

3. One of the best accounts is still that of Henry Adams in his classic *History of the United States during the Administrations of Thomas Jefferson and James Madison* (New York: Library of America, 1986) [first published in 1889–91], II, 993–1032. But see also James Chace and Caleb Carr, *America Invulnerable: The Quest for Absolute Security from 1812 to Star Wars* (New York: Summit Books, 1988), pp. 17–40; and Donald R. Hickey, *The War of 1812: A Forgotten Conflict* (Urbana: University of Illinois Press, 1989), pp. 195–204.

4. I am indebted to my Yale student Justin Zaremby for reminding me of this lurid verse.

5. Chace and Carr, *America Invulnerable,* p. 37. Emphasis added.

6. Jean Bethke Elshtain first suggested this idea to me. But see also Chace and Carr, *America Invulnerable,* pp. 318–19.

7. "Observations Concerning the Increase of Mankind," in Leonard W. Labaree, ed., *The Papers of Benjamin Franklin* (New Haven: Yale University Press, 1961), IV, 233. See also Edmund S. Morgan, *Benjamin Franklin* (New Haven: Yale University Press, 2002), pp. 75–76. Thomas Paine made the point about islands and continents explicit in his great 1776 pamphlet *Common Sense.*

8. *The Federalist* (New York: Modern Library, n.d.), p. 61.

9. For Jefferson's continentalism, see Robert W. Tucker and David C. Hendrickson, *Empire of Liberty: The Statecraft of Thomas Jefferson* (New York: Oxford University Press, 1990), pp. 87–171.

10. Ibid., pp. 175–228. See also, on the origins of the War of 1812, Bradford Perkins, *Prologue to War: England and the United States, 1805–1812* (Berkeley: University of California Press, 1961); and J. C. A. Stagg, *Mr. Madison's War: Politics, Diplomacy, and Warfare in the Early American Republic, 1783–1830* (Princeton: Princeton University Press, 1983).

11. George Dangerfield, *The Awakening of American Nationalism, 1815–1828* (New York: Harper & Row, 1965), p. 4.

12. The best explanation of Adams's strategy is still Samuel Flagg Bemis's classic *John Quincy Adams and the Foundations of American Foreign Policy* (New York: Knopf, 1949). But see also William Earl Weeks, *John Quincy Adams and American Global Empire* (Lexington: University Press of Kentucky, 1992). During the nuclear era the terms "preemption" and "prevention" took on a distinctive meaning. Pre-

emption implied military action undertaken to forestall an imminent attack from a hostile state. Prevention implied starting a war to keep such a state from building the capability to attack. For more on the distinction, see Richard Betts, *Surprise Attack: Lessons for Defense Planning* (Washington: Brookings, 1982), pp. 145–47. For the 19th century, though, when communications were slow, weapons had not yet achieved the capacity for mass destruction, not all adversaries functioned as states, and attacks could as often take the form of raids as of invasions, the distinction between preemption and prevention seems to me to blur. I have therefore used the term "preemption" throughout this chapter.

13. Adams to George W. Erving, November 28, 1818, quoted in Bemis, *John Quincy Adams,* p. 327. See also Weeks, *John Quincy Adams,* pp. 104–46.

14. Quoted in ibid., p. 57. The case in question involved what Adams called "piratical establishments" on Amelia and Galveston islands.

15. Quoted in Thomas R. Hietala, *Manifest Design: Anxious Aggrandizement in Late Jacksonian America* (Ithaca: Cornell University Press, 1985), pp. 136–37.

16. Weeks, *John Quincy Adams,* pp. 193–94.

17. For Jackson's policy on Indian removals, see Sean Michael O'Brien, *In Bitterness and in Tears: Andrew Jackson's Destruction of the Creeks and Seminoles* (New York: Praeger, 2003).

18. Norman A. Graebner, *Empire on the Pacific: A Study in American Continental Expansion* (New York: Ronald Press, 1955). See also Hietala, *Manifest Design,* which emphasizes fears that the British might use Texas as a base from which to promote the abolition of slavery as a motive for American annexation.

19. Anders Stephanson, *Manifest Destiny: American Expansion and the Empire of Right* (New York: Hill and Wang, 1995), pp. 59–61.

20. For a similar argument, see Walter A. McDougall, *Promised Land, Crusader State: The American Encounter with the World since 1776* (Boston: Houghton Mifflin, 1997), pp. 77–78. Adams himself, with respect to Florida, had strongly endorsed the Congressional "No Transfer" Resolution of 1811, which had insisted that the United States could not, "without serious inquietitude, see any part of the said territory pass into the hands of any foreign power" except Spain. (Weeks, *John Quincy Adams,* pp. 27–28, 65–67.)

21. The Naval Historical Center's assessment is at: http://www.history.navy.mil/faqs/faq71–1.htm.

22. David F. Trask, *The War with Spain in 1898* (Lincoln: University of Nebraska Press, 1997); Ivan Musicant, *Empire by Default: The Spanish-American War and the Dawn of the American Century* (New York: Henry Holt, 1998).

23. Quoted in McDougall, *Promised Land, Crusader State,* p. 115.

24. For American intervention in the Caribbean, Central America,

and Mexico, see David Healy, *Drive to Hegemony: The United States in the Caribbean, 1898–1917* (Madison: University of Wisconsin Press, 1988); Max Boot, *The Savage Wars of Peace: Small Wars and the Rise of American Power* (New York: Basic Books, 2002).

25. George W. Bush address at the United States Military Academy, West Point, New York, June 1, 2002, available at: http://www .whitehouse.gov/news/releases/2002/06.

26. Quoted in McDougall, *Promised Land, Crusader State,* p. 44. For the possible influence on Washington's Farewell Address, see Bemis, *John Quincy Adams,* pp. 62–65.

27. Weeks, *John Quincy Adams,* pp. 147–75.

28. Bemis, *John Quincy Adams,* pp. 382–84.

29. Quoted in ibid., p. 385. See also Dexter Perkins, *A History of the Monroe Doctrine* (Boston: Little, Brown, 1963).

30. McDougall, *Promised Land, Crusader State,* pp. 40–42, 50.

31. Robert Kagan, *Of Paradise and Power: America and Europe in the New World Order* (New York: Knopf, 2003), pp. 43–46; Richard Crockatt, *America Embattled: September 11, Anti-Americanism, and the Global Order* (New York: Routledge, 2003), pp. 142–46.

32. John Quincy Adams to Abigail Adams, June 30, 1811, quoted in Bemis, *John Quincy Adams,* p. 182.

33. Adams to the Monroe Cabinet, November 16, 1819, quoted in ibid., p. 367.

34. Reginald C. Stuart, *United States Expansion and British North America, 1775–1871* (Chapel Hill: University of North Carolina Press, 1988), documents this process.

35. See Hietala, *Manifest Design,* pp. 133–72.

36. Boot, *The Savage Wars of Peace,* pp. 99–128, makes the point, though, that the American counterinsurgency effort in the Philippines was successful.

37. Adams address, July 4, 1821, quoted in Perkins, *The Creation of a Republican Empire,* pp. 149–50.

38. McDougall, *Promised Land, Crusader* State, p. 97; Chace and Carr, *America Invulnerable,* pp. 117–21; Alfred Jackson Hanna and Kathryn Abbey Hanna, *Napoleon III and Mexico: American Triumph over Monarchy* (Chapel Hill: University of North Carolina Press, 1971).

39. For the Cuban exception, see Gaddis Smith, *The Last Years of the Monroe Doctrine, 1945–1993* (New York: Hill and Wang, 1994), pp. 91–112.

40. Olney to Thomas F. Bayard, July 20, 1895, in Norman Graebner, ed., *Ideas and Diplomacy: Readings in the Intellectual Tradition of American Foreign Policy* (New York: Oxford University Press, 1964), p. 254.

41. I have borrowed, here and elsewhere, a term made famous by Melvyn P. Leffler in his book *A Preponderance of Power: National Security, the Truman Administration, and the Cold War* (Stanford: Stanford University Press, 1992). Leffler links this Cold War concept to the con-

duct of post-Cold War American foreign policy in his 2003 Harmsworth Inaugural Lecture at the University of Oxford.

42. Bush West Point speech, June 1, 2002.

43. My argument here parallels that of Walter Russell Mead's recent book, *Special Providence: American Foreign Policy and How It Changed the World* (New York: Knopf, 2001), which identifies several distinct American foreign policy traditions that have persisted since the early days of the republic. Mead's most original contribution, though—the identification of a "Jacksonian school"—in my view underestimates the influence of John Quincy Adams.

## 3. THE TWENTIETH CENTURY

1. A point eloquently made by Jean Bethke Elshtain, *Just War against Terror: The Burden of American Power in a Violent World* (New York: Basic Books, 2003), p. 10.

2. Speech to the Congress of the United States, September 20, 2001, http://www.whitehouse.gov/news/releases/2001/09/200109 20-8.html.

3. For a fellow grand strategist's appreciation of FDR, see Henry Kissinger, *Diplomacy* (New York: Simon and Schuster, 1994), pp. 369–93.

4. James Boswell, *Life of Johnson,* edited by R. W. Chapman (New York: Oxford University Press, 1998), p. 849.

5. Frank Ninkovich describes these clashing perceptions of secu-

rity requirements, as well as Wilson's thinking on the indivisibility of security, in *Modernity and Power: A History of the Domino Theory in the Twentieth Century* (Chicago: University of Chicago Press, 1994), pp. 1–68.

6. Lloyd E. Ambrosius, *Woodrow Wilson and the American Diplomatic Tradition: The Treaty Fight in Perspective* (New York: Cambridge University Press, 1987); John Milton Cooper, *Breaking the Heart of the World: Woodrow Wilson and the Fight for the League of Nations* (New York: Cambridge University Press, 2001).

7. Dana G. Munro, *The United States and the Caribbean Republics, 1921–1933* (Princeton: Princeton University Press, 1974).

8. Robert H. Ferrell, *American Diplomacy in the Great Depression: Hoover-Stimson Foreign Policy, 1929–1933* (New York: Norton, 1969).

9. Robert Dallek, *Franklin D. Roosevelt and American Foreign Policy, 1932–1945* (New York: Oxford University Press, 1979), pp. 101–68. See also Barbara Rearden Farnham, *Roosevelt and the Munich Crisis: A Study of Political Decision-making* (Princeton: Princeton University Press, 1997).

10. Roosevelt address to Congress, September 21, 1939, in Samuel I. Rosenman, ed., *The Public Papers and Addresses of Franklin D. Roosevelt: 1939* (New York: Macmillan, 1941), p. 515.

11. The diary of Secretary of War Henry L. Stimson, for example, in the Manuscript and Archives Division of the Sterling Memorial Library at Yale University, is filled with expressions of this nature.

12. The most thorough recent critique is Frederick W. Marks III, *Wind over Sand: The Diplomacy of Franklin D. Roosevelt* (Athens: University of Georgia Press, 1988).

13. A. J. P. Taylor, *English History, 1914–1945* (New York: Oxford University Press, 1965), p. 577. This discussion of FDR's grand strategy draws on what I've said about him in three earlier books: *The United States and the Origins of the Cold War, 1941–1947* (New York: Columbia University Press, 1972); *Strategies of Containment: A Critical Appraisal of Postwar American National Security Policy* (New York: Oxford University Press, 1982); and *We Now Know: Rethinking Cold War History* (New York: Oxford University Press, 1997).

14. David Reynolds, *From Munich to Pearl Harbor: Roosevelt's America and the Origins of the Second World War* (Chicago: Ivan R. Dee, 2001), pp. 89, 170.

15. McGeorge Bundy, *Danger and Survival: Choices about the Bomb in the First Fifty Years* (New York: Random House, 1988), pp. 3–53, provides a fine discussion of FDR's remarkable decision to build the atomic bomb.

16. Milovan Djilas, *Conversations with Stalin*, trans. Michael B. Petrovich (New York: Harcourt, Brace & World, 1962), p. 114.

17. Mark A. Stoler provides the best recent discussion of these alternatives in *Allies and Adversaries: The Joint Chiefs of Staff, the Grand Alliance, and U.S. Strategy in World War II* (Chapel Hill: University of North Carolina Press, 2000).

18. Eisenhower to Marshall, April 23, 1945, quoted in Forrest C. Pogue, *The Supreme Command: United States Army in World War II: The European Theater of Operations* (Washington: Government Printing Office, 1954), p. 486.

19. Reynolds, *From Munich to Pearl Harbor*, pp. 162–63.

20. The distinction, as noted earlier, is that preemption implies military action undertaken to forestall an imminent attack from a hostile state. Prevention implies starting a war to keep such a state from building the capability to attack.

21. The account that follows draws on my own *Strategies of Containment*.

22. Michael J. Hogan, *The Marshall Plan: America, Britain, and the Reconstruction of Western Europe, 1947–1952* (New York: Cambridge University Press, 1987), pp. 427–30.

23. Kennan explains his reasoning in his *Memoirs: 1925–1950* (Boston: Atlantic Little, Brown, 1967), pp. 339–43.

24. Gaddis, *We Now Know*, pp. 198–203.

25. Ibid., p. 91.

26. Ibid., pp. 88–92, 103–110, 230–34. Marc Trachtenberg has argued that Eisenhower's NATO strategy did contemplate a preemptive nuclear strike against Soviet targets upon evidence that war was imminent, but he also notes that Kennedy, by 1963, had explicitly rejected such a strategy. See Trachtenberg's discussion of the 1954 NATO document MC-48 in *A Constructed Peace: The Making of the European Set-*

*tlement, 1945–1963* (Princeton: Princeton University Press, 1999), pp. 156–78, 182–3.

27. For the importance of the Pearl Harbor analogy in the thinking of Kennedy and his advisers, see Ernest R. May and Philip D. Zelikow, eds., *The Kennedy Tapes: Inside the White House during the Cuban Missile Crisis* (Cambridge, Massachusetts: Harvard University Press, 1997), especially pp. 3–4, 121, 143, 189, 196, 207, 234, 244.

28. I owe this "something worse" principle to George F. Kennan, who got it from Hilaire Belloc's poem about the unfortunate "Jim" (who was eaten by a lion) in his *Cautionary Tales:* "And always keep a-hold of Nurse / For fear of finding something worse."

29. For a sophisticated development of this argument, see G. John Ikenberry, *After Victory: Institutions, Strategic Restraint, and the Rebuilding of Order after Major Wars* (Princeton: Princeton University Press, 2001).

30. *Le Monde,* September 12, 2001.


4. THE TWENTY-FIRST CENTURY

1. See, for example, Fyodor Dostoevski, *Devils,* also translated as *The Possessed* (1871); and Joseph Conrad, *The Secret Agent* (1907).

2. Commencement address, United States Military Academy, West Point, New York, June 1, 2002, available on the White House website: http://www.whitehouse.gov.

3. For assessments of American predominance in the post-Cold War

world, see Joseph S. Nye, Jr., *Bound to Lead: The Changing Nature of American Power* (New York: Basic Books, 1990); and, more recently, G. John Ikenberry, ed., *America Unrivaled: The Future of the Balance of Power* (Ithaca: Cornell University Press, 2002).

4. This report appeared in three stages: *New World Coming: American Security in the 21st Century* (September 15, 1999), *Seeking a National Strategy: A Concert for Preserving Security and Promoting Freedom* (April 15, 2000), and *Road Map for National Security: Imperative for Change* (March 15, 2001).

5. The standard account is Roberta Wohlstetter, *Pearl Harbor: Warning and Decision* (Stanford: Stanford University Press, 1962).

6. Or so I've argued in *The Landscape of History: How Historians Map the Past* (New York: Oxford University Press, 2002), especially Chapter 4.

7. Strobe Talbott, *The Russia Hand: A Memoir of Presidential Diplomacy* (New York: Random House, 2002), p. 131. For the "engagement and enlargement" strategy, see Lake's September 21, 1993, address at Johns Hopkins University, at: http://www.mtholyoke.edu/acad/intrel/lakedoc.html. Francis Fukuyama's ideas appeared first as "The End of History," *The National Interest,* 16 (Summer, 1989), 3–18, and then more fully as *The End of History and the Last Man* (New York: Free Press, 1992).

8. It's significant that Henry Kissinger felt it necessary, as the

Clinton administration left office, to publish a book entitled *Does America Need a Foreign Policy? Toward a Diplomacy for the Twenty-First Century* (New York: Simon and Schuster, 2001). In it he warned (p. 19) against "the temptation of acting as if the United States needed no long-range foreign policy at all and could confine itself to a case-by-case response to challenges as they arise."

9. For one non-rocket scientist's anticipation of this result, see John Lewis Gaddis, *The United States and the End of the Cold War: Implications, Reconsiderations, Provocations* (New York: Oxford University Press, 1992), pp. 193–216.

10. See Joseph E. Stiglitz, *Globalization and Its Discontents* (New York: Norton, 2002); also Amy Chua, *World on Fire: How Exporting Free Market Democracy Breeds Ethnic Hatred and Global Instability* (New York: Doubleday, 2003).

11. John Lewis Gaddis, "Living in Candlestick Park," *Atlantic Monthly,* 283 (April 1999), 65–74.

12. For a map showing new American bases in the region, see the *New York Times,* April 20, 2003, p. B5.

13. The tendency to underrate Bush has been particularly pronounced among American and European academics. This no doubt has something to do with their predominantly liberal political orientation; but it may also reflect the extent to which university education these days tilts toward professional specialization. It too easily follows

from this, then, that generalists—like Bush—are lightweights. For more on this point, see Eliot A. Cohen, *Supreme Command: Soldiers, Statesmen, and Leadership in Wartime* (New York: Free Press, 2002), p. xiii.

14. The West Point speech and the National Security Strategy statement are on the White House website: http://www.whitehouse.gov.

15. Bush NSS, p. iv.

16. Clinton NSS preface, available at: http://clinton2.nara.gov/WH/ EOP/NSC/html/documents/ nssrpref.html. Both the Bush and Clinton statements respond to congressional mandate, included in the Goldwater-Nichols Act of 1986, which requires the president to report periodically on national security strategy.

17. Bush NSS, pp. 13–14.

18. Bush NSS, p. 15.

19. Bush NSS, p. v.

20. Bob Woodward, *Bush at War* (New York: Simon and Schuster, 2002), p. 30, discusses the origins of this doctrine. For the NSS restatement of it, see p. 5.

21. Bush NSS, p. 15. The NSS does not, however, explicitly make the connection I do to the Adams precedent.

22. Bush NSS, pp. 6, 15.

23. Bush NSS, pp. iv, 30.

24. Bush West Point speech, June 1, 2002. This passage constitutes formal approval of a controversial recommendation by Paul Wolfowitz, deputy secretary of defense in the current Bush administration, in a

1992 "Defense Planning Guidance" draft, subsequently leaked to the press and disavowed by the George H. W. Bush administration. For more on Wolfowitz, see Bill Keller, "The Sunshine Warrior," *New York Times Magazine,* September 22, 2002.

25. See, for example, William C. Wohlforth, "The Stability of a Unipolar World," *International Security,* 24 (Summer, 1999), 5–41; G. John Ikenberry, *After Victory: Institutions, Strategic Restraint, and the Rebuilding of Order after Major Wars* (Princeton: Princeton University Press, 2001); Stephen G. Brooks and William C. Wohlforth, "American Primacy in Perspective," *Foreign Affairs,* 81 (July/August, 2002), 20–33.

26. Bush West Point speech, June 1, 2002. Robert Kagan's *Of Paradise and Power: America and Europe in the New World Order* (New York: Knopf, 2003) describes one part of the world—Europe—where such a situation already exists.

27. Bush West Point speech, June 1, 2002; Bush NSS, p. 3.

28. See, for example, Fouad Ajami, *Dream Palace of the Arabs: A Generation's Odyssey* (New York: Vintage, 1999); Bernard Lewis, *What Went Wrong? Western Impact and Middle Eastern Response* (New York: Oxford University Press, 2002) and *The Crisis of Islam: Holy War and Unholy Terror* (New York: Modern Library, 2003); as well as Gilles Kepel, *Jihad: The Trail of Political Islam* (Cambridge, Massachusetts: Harvard University Press, 2002); Paul Berman, *Terror and Liberalism* (New York: Norton, 2003), especially pp. 52–120; and Fareed Zakaria,

*The Future of Freedom: Illiberal Democracy at Home and Abroad* (New York: Norton, 2003), especially pp. 119–59; all of which stress the extent to which Islamic rage directed against the West is a relatively recent phenomenon, linked to the frustrations of having been left behind by the processes of modernization. For an Arab assessment, see the *Arab Human Development Report: Creating Opportunities for Future Generations* (New York: United Nations, 2002).

29. Bush NSS, p. 6.

30. For more on this, see John Lewis Gaddis, "And Now This: Lessons from the Old Era for the New One," in Strobe Talbott and Nayan Chanda, eds., *The Age of Terror: America and the World after September 11th* (New York: Basic Books, 2001), pp. 13–14.

31. Joshua Muravchik, "The Bush Manifesto," *Commentary,* 114 (December 2002), 28–29, emphasizes this point. Philip Zelikow has suggested to me that this conservative optimism stems in part from the experience of several top Bush administration aides who witnessed the end of the Cold War as members of the George H. W. Bush administration. His own book *Germany United and Europe Transformed: A Study in Statecraft* (Cambridge, Massachusetts: Harvard University Press, 1995), co-authored with Condoleeza Rice, documents the experience. The Wilson-Reagan connection is best described in a book by someone else not normally thought of as a Wilsonian, Henry Kissinger, *Diplomacy* (New York: Simon and Schuster, 1994).

32. Bush State of the Union address, January 29, 2002, available

at: http://www.whitehouse.gov /news/releases/2002/01/20020129–11.html. For the drafting of this address, see David Frum, *The Right Man: The Surprise Presidency of George W. Bush* (New York: Random House, 2003).

33. The argument is clearly advanced, with respect to Iraq, in John J. Mearsheimer and Stephen M. Walt, "An Unnecessary War," *Foreign Policy,* 134 (January/February, 2003), 50–59. For the alternative viewpoint, see Kenneth M. Pollack, *The Threatening Storm: The Case for Invading Iraq* (New York: Random House, 2002).

34. John King, "Bush Calls Saddam 'the guy who tried to kill my dad,'" *CNN Inside Politics,* September 27, 2002, at: http://www.cnn.com/2002/ALLPOLITICS/09/27/bush.war.talk/. See also Woodward, *Bush at War,* pp. 84–85.

35. Bush NSS, p. 31. It is, perhaps, no accident that the Department of Defense at the end of 2002 was distributing free copies of *Henry V,* as well as other classics, to troops preparing for action against Iraq. See Ben Macintyre, "The Great Novelists Not Fit for Duty in This War of Words," *London Times,* December 28, 2002. I am indebted to my former Yale student Chad Golder for this reference. For the "clash of civilizations" thesis, see Samuel P. Huntington, *The Clash of Civilizations and the Remaking of World Order* (New York: Simon and Schuster, 1996).

36. Bush United Nations speech, September 12, 2002, http://www.whitehouse.gov/news/releases /2002/09/20020912–1.html.

37. See, for example, John Charmley's controversial portrayal of Churchill as a failed grand strategist, *Churchill: The End of Glory: A Political Biography* (New York: Harcourt, 1993).

38. "[N]o nation can build a safer, better world alone. Alliances and multilateral institutions can multiply the strength of freedom-loving nations." (Bush NSS, p. vi.)

39. The Bush administration was forced to acknowledge, in July 2003, that the President's State of the Union address six months earlier had included inaccurate information about alleged Iraqi purchases of uranium from Niger. For two hypotheses about what happened to Iraqi weapons of mass destruction, see Bob Drogin, "The Vanishing: What Happened to the WMD?" *The New Republic,* July 21, 2003, pp. 20–24; and Michael R. Gordon, "Weapons of Mass Confusion," *New York Times,* August 1, 2003.

40. For the origins and conduct of the war in Iraq, see the International Institute for Strategic Studies, *Strategic Survey 2002/3* (London: IISS, 2003), pp. 145–58.

41. See note 22.

42. The original source was Harlan Ullman, James P. Wade, L. A. Edney, *Shock and Awe: Achieving Rapid Dominance* (Washington: National Defense University Institute for Strategic Studies, 1996).

43. For Bush's own thinking on this point, see Woodward, *Bush at War,* p. 81. The argument here parallels the one the Israelis have used

to justify pulling down houses in Palestinian neighborhoods that harbor suicide bombers.

44. See Chapter 2.

45. The best brief treatment of Bismarck's strategy is still Henry A. Kissinger, "The White Revolutionary: Reflections on Bismarck," *Daedalus,* 97 (Summer, 1968), 888–924.

46. I have in mind here the administration's unnecessarily harsh rhetoric in stating its opposition to the Kyoto Protocol on Climate Change, the International Criminal Court, and the Comprehensive Test Ban Treaty, as well as its failure to clarify the legal status of Al Qaeda and Taliban prisoners captured in Afghanistan and incarcerated at the Guantanamo Naval Base in Cuba.

47. I should like to thank my student Sulmaan Khan for having pushed me to consider this question.

48. Huntington, *The Clash of Civilizations and the Remaking of World Order,* p. 21.

49. See note 35.

50. See, for example, *The Federalist No. 1,* by Alexander Hamilton, which warned that "of those men who have overturned the liberties of republics, the greatest number have begun their career by paying an obsequious court to the people; commencing demagogues, and ending tyrants." (*The Federalist* [New York: Modern Library, n.d.], pp. 5–6.)

51. Zakaria, *The Future of Freedom,* passim. See also, on this last

point, Robert A. Dahl, *On Democracy* (New Haven: Yale University Press, 1998).

52. For a withering review, see Robert Kagan, "The Great Unwashed: Why Democracy Must Remain America's Goal Abroad," *The New Republic,* 229 (July 7 and 14, 2003), 27–37.

53. I have stolen this definition from John Lewis Gaddis, *We Now Know: Rethinking Cold War History* (New York: Oxford University Press, 1997), p. 27.

54. See, on this point, Zakaria, *The Future of Freedom,* p. 57; also Niall Ferguson, *Empire: The Rise and Demise of the British World Order and the Lessons for Global Power* (New York: Basic Books, 2003).

55. The Spring 2003 issue of *The National Interest* contains several contributions to this debate. See also Andrew J. Bacevich, *American Empire: The Realities and Consequences of U.S. Diplomacy* (Cambridge, Massachusetts: Harvard University Press, 2002).

56. See Robert W. Tucker and David C. Hendrickson, *Empire of Liberty: The Statecraft of Thomas Jefferson* (New York: Oxford University Press, 1990); also Anders Stephanson, *Manifest Destiny: American Expansion and the Empire of Right* (New York: Hill and Wang, 1995).

57. For more on this, see Geir Lundestad's insightful *The American "Empire" and Other Studies of US Foreign Policy in a Comparative Perspective* (New York: Oxford University Press, 1990).

58. Adam Smith, *An Inquiry into the Nature and Causes of the Wealth of Nations* (New York: Modern Library, 2000), p. 672.

59. *The Federalist,* p. 146.

60. I have discussed the functioning of this system at greater length in *We Now Know,* pp. 191–203.

61. For a broader set of historical models aimed at producing similar results, see Robert D. Kaplan, "Supremacy by Stealth: Ten Rules for Managing the World," *The Atlantic,* 292 (July–August, 2003), 65–83.

## 5. AN EVENING AT YALE

1. The phrase is from Lincoln's Second Annual Message to Congress, December 1, 1862.

2. Thomas L. Friedman, "9/11 Lesson Plan," *New York Times,* September 4, 2002, makes this argument, drawing on an essay by Larry Miller in the January 14, 2002, issue of *The Weekly Standard.*

## INDEX

Roosevelt, Franklin Delano *(continued)*
preemption and, 38–39, 54–58, 61;
pre-war passivity and, 45; response
to Pearl Harbor, 31, 35–37, 65
Roosevelt, Theodore, 20–21
Rudman, Warren, 74. *See also* Hart-
Rudman report
Russell, Bertrand, 62
Russia, 90, 97. *See also* Soviet Union

Saudi Arabia, 82, 97
security, American sense of: American
character and, 7–10; geographic iso-
lation and, 39–40, 46; impact of
September 11th on, 72–73; security
elsewhere and, 42–43, 44, 110–111.
*See also* security through expansion
security threats: European powers as,
16, 17, 18–21, 23–24, 26–27, 29, 39;
Hart-Rudman report and, 73–74, 75;
1990s American complacency and,
76–80, 85, 90; non-state actors as,
16, 17, 18, 69–75, 84–85; pre-World
War II, 41–46. *See also* terrorists
security through expansion: American
response to threats and, 12–13, 32–
33, 37; arrogance and, 110–111, 113;
development of tradition, 16–30,
108–109; elements of strategy for,
15–16, 37–38; federalism and, 112–
113; founding fathers and, 13–15;
roots of "empire of liberty" idea and,
107–109. *See also* continental hegemony; global hegemony; hegemony;

preemption; unilateralism; American
sense of security
self-determination, 77, 78
September 11th: as attack on hope,
115–116; costs vs. results of, 72; effects of Bush response to, 80–83;
hegemony and, 66–67, 100; impacts
of, 2–5, 9–10, 70–72; nature of adversary and, 69–71; reasons for total
surprise of, 74–80; security traditions in response to, 16, 30–31, 37–
38; weakness of states and, 80
shock and awe: in Bush strategy, 98–
101; consolidation and reassurance
and, 101–103
Smith, Adam, 111–112, 113
"something worse" principle, 53, 63–
64, 65–67, 109, 131n; Bush strategy
and, 100–101, 110
sovereignty, 28–29, 108; Bush Doctrine
and, 86, 109–110
Soviet Union: containment strategy
and, 59; FDR's cooperation with, 47,
55; Marshall Plan and, 60–61, 66;
preemption against, 54–58; spheres
of influence and, 55, 61; spread of
democracy to, 76. *See also* Russia
Spanish Florida, 17, 19, 56, 124n
spheres of influence: asymmetry of legitimacy and, 64–65; Cold War expansion of, 58–65; continental hegemony and, 28–30; pre-World War II
views of extent of, 39–46; sovereignty and, 28–29, 108; World War II
expansion of, 38–39, 46–58, 109.